Rise Above the Cloud
With
Digital Marketing

MICHAEL PAULE and SHELLY DUBOW

Register for FREE Bonus Content

* Scan this QR Code to Register for the FREE Book Bonuses
* Or Visit http://0s4.com/r/MRK3B4
* Or Text **Bookbonus** to 58885
* Or Text your name & email address to 1 (805) 601-8001

http://www.RiseAboveTheCloud.net

DISCLAIMER

The information in this book is distributed on an "as is" basis, without warranty. While every precaution has been taken in the preparation of this book, neither of the authors or publisher shall have any liability to any person or entity with respect to any liability, loss, or damage caused or alleged to be caused directly or indirectly by the information or websites contained in this book.

Throughout this book, trademarked names are used. Rather than put a trademark symbol in every occurrence of a trademarked name, we are using the names only in an editorial fashion and to the benefit of the trademark owner or with no intention of infringement of the trademark. Where those designations appear in this book, the designations have been printed in initial caps.

The Internet is an ever changing medium and websites change all the time. All links and recommendations herein are for informational purposes only and are not warranted for content, accuracy or any other implied or explicit purpose. The ideas and opinions express in this book are those of the authors and there are no guarantees that you will have success with them. Every attempt was made to find typos and grammatical errors but if you discover any, please forward them to info@mobiledata360.com

TABLE OF CONTENTS

TESTIMONIALS

"If you want to know the current state of Mobile Marketing . . . and how to master it, your answers are in this book. These guys know what they are doing"

Martan Mann,
Jazz Skills for Piano

"Those who need a crash course would be well advised to pick up "Rise Above the Cloud with Digital Marketing". The book will give them all the basics they need about Podcasting, Book Publishing, Video Marketing, Social Marketing and Mobile Marketing".

Ned Raynolds
Principal
The Dilenschneider Group, Inc.

"Well done...the information described within certainly helps to unfold the challenge and projects to the reader, not only the benefits, but a clear road to achieving those benefits as well"

Richard Levin
Chairman
Private Investors Forum

"As the director of business development for a medical software company we have been exploring digital marketing to promote our products. It was timely that I came across "Rise Above the Cloud with Digital Marketing" as it solidified research we conducted on the subject and validated that our time was well spent. Like any developing venue there are hurdles to understanding the right path to take. "Rise Above the Cloud with Digital Marketing" provides great direction and insight on not only the importance of digital marketing to a business's marketing efforts but also insight into planning a campaign and the elements to address up front in content

and execution. There is good statistical insight to the benefits of digital marketing that validated our thinking to take advantage of this promotional resource. If you're looking into digital marketing for your business, this is a must read"

Stephen C. Holmes
Director of Business Development
Patient Now

"Rise Above the Cloud with Digital Marketing" gives the reader a comprehensive understanding of how to go about marketing in this amazing digital world in which we live. The writing is very easy to follow; yet it's best to have your tablet ready for digital note taking because of the vast amount of usable information you will want to retain. Life long learning is essential, especially in the world of technology. Mike Paule and Shelly Dubow have gifted us with an incredible marketing manual which you will need to keep close for years to come."

Jill Shaffer
Executive Director
Ventura County Leadership Academy

"As a small business owner, I found Rise Above the Cloud With Digital Marketing to be well written and informative. Real estate is a relationship business. Rise Above the Cloud With Digital Marketing gave me several actionable ideas that will have a direct positive impact on my business. Mike and Shelly clearly have a good understanding of the importance of relationship building and its importance to the success of any relationship based business. Rise Above the Cloud With Digital Marketing is mandatory reading for anybody who wants to build a successful relationship based business!"

Tom Bregman
Broker/Owner of Bregman Properties

ACKNOWLEDGEMENTS

Michael Paule

Publishing my first book would not have been possible without the support of many family, friends and colleagues.

Thank you to Robin Paule, and to my two beautiful daughters, Melissa and Kelsey, who are always such an inspiration to me. To my friends and colleagues on the various councils, boards and non-profit organizations in which I serve, thank you for your input and support to help make this book a big success.

Thank you to Tom and Janet Bregman, Jill Shaffer and all my friends in the Oak Park, California community who continually support me in my business, community and personal endeavors and provide honest and timely feedback.

Thank you to my friends in the social media universe, who support one another and have provided valuable suggestions with regards to this book.

Thank you to my brother and sister (Dr. Lawrence and Pamela), and Dad (Herb Paule), a truly amazing man, who reminds me what hard work, dedication and commitment, is all about. I love you.

To my Mother (Joyce Paule) who passed away last Fall after a valiant fight with cancer, thank you for all that you did for me over the years and for your constant love and support. This book is dedicated to you.

To the memory of my cousin, Ken Nemeroff and Aunt Rene Raatjes.

Thank you for so many wonderful years of memories. We all miss you greatly.

And to my co-author, long-time friend and business colleague, Shelly Dubow. Thank you for your friendship, advice and support for all these years. I can't thank you enough for always being there for me and for your willingness to jump in and provide your time, expertise, knowledge and talents to help keep me focused to make this book a big success.

Shelly Dubow

I would like to extend my gratitude to everyone who helped me in the preparation of the information that I contributed to this book. As a co-author, this was my first writing venture into one of the most topical business categories today. As a result, I can now appreciate and understand the hours and rigors of sifting through thousands of pages of research and information in order to present concise viewpoints and recommendations on the subject matter being discussed in this book.

Thank you to my daughter Lauren, who is a marketing superstar in her own right. She encouraged me to write the material as if I were talking to my best friend rather than to a classroom of students. She knows how passionate I can become when it comes to subjects I really get excited about. I guess that's the parental side of me.

I want to thank my good friends Ned Raynolds, from the Dilenschneider Group, Inc. in New York and Martan Mann from Boulder Creek, CA. for their support. As an editor himself, Ned made several recommendations that I enthusiastically incorporated while Martan, who is a brilliant pianist, teacher and publisher, has already reaped the benefits of Mobile Marketing by utilizing our strategies in his ground breaking online music courses, *"Jazz Skills for Piano"*.

I want to thank my good friend and long time business associate, Steve Holmes, Director of Business Development at Patient Now in Greenwood Village, CO. Over the years Steve has always been a strong advocate of mine. His marketing expertise and business development skills have been both motivating and inspirational.

A special thank you to Richard Levine, Chairman of The Private Investor Forum. As one of the most knowledgeable and successful Venture Capitalists I know, his input on presenting the information and facts in this book so that readers can "cut to the chase" was invaluable.

Mike and I want to extend our thanks to Mike Koenigs, Paul Colligan, and Ed Rush from the Pulse Network in San Diego. It was their encouragement and insistence that we follow our passion for Digital Marketing by writing and publishing this book. As marketers and publishers themselves, their expertise in this venue was extremely helpful.

And finally, a very special thanks to my good friend, long time business associate and co-author Mike Paule. We have known each other for over 20 years and he never seizes to amaze me. His knowledge, business skills and entrepreneurial experience combined with his dedication to his family and to his many civic duties, makes me so proud to be his partner in this venture. I look forward to this being the first of many projects in the future.

ABOUT THE AUTHORS

Michael Paule

As a successful entrepreneur with nearly 30 years of experience in finance, marketing, sales and technology consulting, Mike Paule developed relationships with some of the leading companies and organizations in the Country, including multiple Fortune 500 companies, many law firms, (Local City, County, State and Federal agencies), healthcare organizations and many others.

After selling his last business in 2011, he started MobileData360, LLC and has generated nearly $6 million in sales in the past few years. Mike is known as an innovator and a pioneer in on-line (cloud-based) solutions for businesses going back to the late 1990s.

Early on in the development of on-line technologies, he recognized the tremendous advantage that these technologies could hold for the business community and has amassed a tremendous amount of expertise in the deployment of cloud-based solutions and marketing strategies.

In his prior venture, he helped businesses large and small go digital with their information management needs and he takes great pride in the long-term business relationships he fostered with many of his customers.

Recognizing the power of mobile technologies and video as an important customer engagement tool, Mike has partnered with some of the leading experts in marketing, video, social media and mobile technologies to offer his customers substantial expertise in helping them harness the power of today's solutions to build or expand their customer base, automate their marketing campaigns and properly develop their online presence.

In addition to his extensive business background, Mike is a passionate and dedicated community leader and currently serves as a local publicly elected official (Councilman and Water District Board Member). He also serves in leadership roles on several non-profit foundations and was recently elected as President of the Ventura County Special Districts Association.

Michael has received a number of awards and recognition for his business success, innovation and community involvement, including being named one of the top 25 most important people in the Conejo Valley (2013), the 2005 Edward M. Masry Integrity in Community Service award and the 2012 recipient of the Golden Acorn award for community service.

Shelly Dubow

Shelly Dubow, a close friend and former business associate of Mike Paule has rejoined with Mike again as Senior Marketing Consultant of MobileData360, LLC.

After having served in the Military, Shelly began his career with Bache & Co, a major member of the New York Stock Exchange. He later joined the Value Line organization in New York as an Executive Vice President and Chief Operating Officer of Value Line Securities, a division of Value Line and The Arnold Bernhard Co.

While at Value Line he created a sales training program utilizing audio and video applications called "Applinetics". This ground breaking sales and marketing program was sponsored by Value Line and widely used by other major Wall Street Securities firms. He later joined the Piedmont Capital organization in California to head up their West Coast securities and insurance marketing operations. There he was responsible for the supervision and sales training of over 160 licensed securities and insurance sales people.

Several years later, as President and CEO of Tristar Oil & Gas, he created a subdivision called "Thermoil" and generated a successful and documented record of more than 8 million dollars of investor profits before selling the company to a major, oil & gas company in Denver, Colorado.

As an inventor, Shelly created the board game of "Qumero" which he licensed to Coleco in New York and Spears Games in England. As a manufacturing entrepreneur in the confectionery industry, he founded the Beverly Hills Confection Collection in Los Angeles and created a unique gourmet product along with an exclusive method of manufacturing it. Prior to selling the company, the award-winning product was distributed throughout airports and up-scale hotels nationwide and exported to Japan.

Throughout his career, Shelly has served as President, Chairman, Director and/or CEO of both public and private companies, which were diversified in a number of fields, including finance, securities arbitration, telecommunications, energy, manufacturing and e-commerce.

FOREWORD

"How can you squander even one more day of not taking advantage of the greatest shifts of our generation? How dare you settle for less when the world has made it so easy for you to be remarkable?" - Seth Godin

The change in marketing tactics and strategies today compared to the last two decades is like trying to compare life at the turn of the 20th Century to today. In other words, there just is no comparison. The impact that digital marketing has had on the world in just a few years has completely and forever changed the way that goods and services interact with consumers and with social media.

With smartphones and tablets leading the way, the tools available to business owners, regardless of their size, have created marketing opportunities that 10 to 15 years ago would have seemed impossible.

The effect that it has had on companies like Google, Amazon, Apple and relative newcomers like Facebook and Twitter has been staggering as billions of people log on to the Internet at least once a day. In Asia alone, over 45% of the population is online. Connecting with those billions of prospective customers would have been a dream just a few years ago.

Today, it is now a daily reality as businesses of all sizes conduct and complete transactions around the world, more and more often on their mobile devices.

Naturally this isn't new news to anyone in the marketing industry including the general public at large. Because of the speed in which this phenomenon has taken placed, even what has been known as the "Baby Boomers" population of older people, they too have now begun to understand, embrace and are participating in the change.

The authors of this book are no strangers to the challenges of adapting over the years to these new marketing realities. Michael and Shelly have been good friends for over 20 years. They have both been entrepreneurs that over the course of their collective careers, spanning more than 30 years, they have created and have successfully presided over business of various sizes and of a diversity of industries. However, both have faced their own unique challenges along this journey.

Mike's Personal Reflection

I began my career after college in the financial services industry and relocated to Southern California in 1986 when the company I was working for in Phoenix, Arizona suddenly went out of business. Shortly after, I accepted a job opportunity to head up a trading department for a securities brokerage firm. After several years, coupled with the challenges facing that industry with the recession in 1991, I joined a startup helping investors navigate the securities arbitration process. After several years and a lot of good and tough lessons learned, I started a technology solutions company (specializing in document imaging and document management technologies) and developed the business from a start-up to around 25 employees at its peak.

Unfortunately, the partners I brought in for the financing side of the business failed to fulfill their obligations and I ended up selling the company and reorganizing it in 2004. At the time of the reorganization, I had about $200,000 of personal debt that I had to contend with, but the revenue from the client base I had developed served to retire that debt in about 12 months (6 months faster than I expected).

I continued to work within that industry as the Marketing Director of the company that I had merged with and enjoyed success in new business development over the subsequent 6 years. When the entrepreneurial bug bit me again, I formed another company and have spent the last several years developing that business, and most importantly devoted countless hours learning and mastering the expertise necessary to succeed. Much like many people out there, I found it necessary to reinvent myself and made sure I had the training and skills to compete at the highest level.

I have certainly had my ups and downs in business and learned some valuable lessons along the way, but it is that experience that has taught me the importance of developing the proper strategy and working with the right experts who keep me focused on what works and where I should be expending my energy and talents.

Shelly's Personal Reflection

I remember when I was in college. I was amazed by the fact that our instructors knew so much about business, yet remained as teachers rather than applying their knowledge and skills by actually going into business for themselves.

I have always believed in that awkward expression "put your money where your mouth is". It is one thing telling someone what to do and how to do it, and even why to do it, when you yourself have never actually done it.

Aside from school teachers, the best example are politicians and elected officials who argue, negotiate and create laws regarding the vast world of business practices yet, many have never run a business, hired a worker or even had to meet a payroll.

"The only vice that cannot be forgiven is hypocrisy. The repentance of a hypocrite is itself hypocrisy."- William Hazlit

I was born and raised in a middle class family in New Jersey. My Dad was a grocer and my Mom was a housewife. Along with my sister Suzanne, who was 5 ½ years younger, we lived in a four-room flat in Irvington until we moved to Newark 15 years later.

Things were tough and money was tight. When I graduated High School, I got a job at Prudential Insurance Company washing walls at night to pay for my tuition at Bloomfield College in New Jersey. After two years at Bloomfield, I joined the Army and really learned what the world was about. When I was discharged, I returned to school and worked part time at several sales jobs.

I was fascinated with the stock market and the world of economics and got a job selling mutual funds. Shortly after, Bache & Co, a major New York stock exchange firm hired me. They sent me to the New York Institute of Finance, a division of NYU for intensive education and training for nearly a year. Upon graduation and with full accreditation, I started to work for my new employer.

After a couple of years, an opportunity came up and I was able to join the Value Line organization in New York as a regional manager. In my new capacity, I created a sales training program utilizing audio and video applications that I called "Applinetics". It became a ground breaking sales and marketing program, and was sponsored by Value Line and widely used by other major Wall Street securities firms. That event led to me being promoted to Executive Vice President and Chief Operating Officer of Value Line Securities, a division of Value Line and The Arnold Bernhard Co.

After several years and longing for warmer weather, I joined the Piedmont Capital organization and with my now growing family, I moved to California to head up their Regional West Coast securities and insurance marketing operations. There I was responsible for the supervision and sales training of over 160 licensed securities and insurance sales people.

Several years later because of my securities experience and new contacts that I made in California, I left Piedmont Capital and became President and CEO of Tristar Oil & Gas, a company engaged in oil & gas exploration. During that time, I joined with another investor group and created a partnership called "Thermoil". Clayton Brokerage of St. Louis underwrote the partnership.

The project generated a successful and documented record of more than 8 million dollars of investor profits, which resulted in my selling the partnership assets to a major, oil & gas Company in Denver, Colorado. Later, I merged Tristar Oil & Gas into Surveyor Industries, a Public Company and took over as Chairman and CEO of the company until I resigned 2 years later to take a sabbatical.

I was feeling invulnerable! Now having the luxury of money and the time to do whatever I wanted I started to explore other avenues of interest.

As an inventor, I created the board game of "Qumero" which through my agent, I licensed to Coleco in New York and Spears

Games in England. Unfortunately, Coleco filed bankruptcy during that time and my game never became what Coleco had hoped it would become. However, I'm told that you can still buy the "Spears" version of the game on the Internet.

Longing for something I could really get excited about, I became enamored with the Fancy Food Industry. As a result, I became a manufacturing entrepreneur in the confectionery industry. I founded the Beverly Hills Confection Collection in Los Angeles and created a unique gourmet product known as the "Truffle Cookie", along with an exclusive method of manufacturing it. Prior to selling the company 6 years later, my award-winning product and packaging was distributed throughout airports and up-scale hotels nationwide including being exported to Japan.

In addition to having been a paid consultant on many projects, I have served as President, Chairman, Director and/or CEO of both public and private companies, which were diversified in a number of fields, including finance, securities arbitration, telecommunications, energy, manufacturing, e-commerce and the toy industry.

It is important to note that by not having the advantages of all the incredible opportunities that are now available with video, audio and mobile marketing including the Internet, I was unable to create a stable steady stream of residual and affiliate income from customer email lists that I would have been able to harvest through various product and service offers. Instead, I was forced to periodically re-invent myself by creating new businesses mostly out of necessity.

Now having immersed myself in the new technologies that have become part of the digital world, I am so excited to combine my business and life experiences into co-authoring this book with Mike

Paule, helping men and women entrepreneurs find that road that will lead them to success and the kind of financial independence that they have always dreamed about.

This book is written and dedicated to serious entrepreneurs who want and need more customers or clients. It is written for those who would like to leverage their experience and "know-how" by using all the aspects of digital marketing in order to build exposure to their product brand or services.

"Rise Above the Cloud with Digital Marketing" will give the reader an overview of each of the major components that make up the world of digital marketing which include Mobile Marketing, Audio and Video Podcasting, Book Publishing, Social Media and Video Marketing. The book will provide the reader a roadmap on how to rise above the "Cloud" and stand out among their competitors. The content in this book will show the reader how to develop credibility, generate leads with a list of email contacts and explain how to build a trustworthy relationship with their clients. It will also include information, guidance and tools that might be most relevant to their business, which can help to create an affinity for their product brand or service.

When it comes to Digital Marketing, it's definitely a new world out there. Business owners and marketers in order to keep up with fast changing trends will need to simply connect, research and put today's continuous stream of data to work for them.

We hope the content of *"Rise Above The Cloud with Digital Marketing"* will provide you with the information and tools that will help put you on the road to becoming a successful author, marketing and business professional.

INTRODUCTION

They say that most people have a story or a book in them that is just waiting to be told. Unfortunately, this notion always seems to be put on permanent hold. Then suddenly, events happen; events that have a profound effect on societies in the way they begin to think, play, communicate and receive information just to name a few. The events become catalysts that give birth to new and seasoned authors who begin to write about the changing complex of what is happening in the world.

We have seen this happen in the sports and entertainment field. We have seen this happen in the world of politics and current events. And now, with the introduction and growing use of smartphones and other mobile devices like tablets and laptops, we are seeing the whole world moving in great numbers to the rapid and vast emerging industry of "Digital Communication".

As a result, we are seeing numerous books available on the subject. Some books cover only single components of the industry like mobile marketing, video and audio, or others that are more comprehensive. The target market for these books has been a growing number of entrepreneurs and businesses. They obviously see this area as a great opportunity to make money.

However, because of the diverse complexity and technical aspects of the industry, knowledge on how to navigate and learn the secrets of why, where, what and how success can be achieved, must still be learned.

This brings us to the question of why the authors of this book felt compelled to join forces at this time to collaborate in conveying their stories and opinions based upon their individual business and life experience?

The answer is simple. Mike Paule and Shelly Dubow, authors of this book, have *"walked the walk and talked the talk"* over 30 years by building a diversity of successful businesses using earlier methods of marketing techniques as well as through modern digital world methods. In that regard, they feel more qualified to better connect with todays growing list of hungry, enthusiastic and aggressive group of entrepreneurs and business people.

Having been there, and through their personal experiences, Mike and Shelly know what challenges our readers are going to be faced with and how to meet them. This is why this book was written and is being dedicated to those men and women who make up the world of entrepreneurs and business people.

STRATEGY 1: VIDEO MARKETING

Introduction

"Innovation distinguishes between a leader and a follower" –
Steve Jobs

The rapidly changing digital landscape has had a dramatic impact on how content is produced and consumed. One of the most significant developments over the past few years is the rapid adoption and use of videos as a strategic marketing tool. Referred to by many as "Video Marketing", one definition is the process of promoting an entity online through the use of carefully crafted, and often short videos that allow individuals, entities or organizations to connect with their audience in a manner much different than through images and text alone.

There are many reasons why video has become such an important tool in a marketer's arsenal. One reason for its popularity is with the rapid adoption of mobile devices, such as smart phones and tablets, coupled with faster connection speeds, it has become much easier to smoothly stream HD quality web video to devices around the Globe.

The popularity of video sharing sites such as YouTube and Vimeo, demonstrate that people love video and according to Google are for more likely to click on a video link on a search result page than they are any text link.

The business of "Video Marketing" has seen extremely rapid growth as the cost and time required to create good quality video has declined significantly making it cost effective for businesses to incorporate this form of content in their marketing implementation.

In this book, we provide a look at the various types of videos that are produced and how they are used to build or enhance a brand for individuals and organizations. At the core of video's popularity is the fact that this form of digital communications allows us to engage with our audience and build a relationship of trust and confidence.

It has been said that relationships are the holy grail of marketing. Why is this important? The reason is that good, loyal customers are ambassadors for your brand and spread your message through their network of contacts. In the past, these relationships were faceless, but digital communications has certainly changed all that and now, marketers can connect with people one-on-one.

Relationships were traditionally formed with face-to-face contact with our friends, neighbors and local organizations, but we can now form similar relationships through the interaction of others using video as a platform. Where once we would visit a trusted resource at a local store for advice on a do-it-yourself project, today we can access a multitude of advice, reviews and other information on Google, Facebook, YouTube and other sites.

The amount of information that can be displayed through one second of video vastly outnumbers the amount of information that can be read. You have probably heard the phrase "a picture is worth a thousand words." With video, you can form an instant emotional connection with an audience and most importantly move them from a simple awareness to a higher level of intimacy.

Through video we are able to recreate the experience of being face-to-face with someone much better than through audio, image or text. Our audience not only hears the message that we are delivering but also gets to experience the physical and verbal expressions that are simply not possible to convey otherwise.

So how important has video become in the digital marketing world? Let's look at some pretty amazing stats that provide solid proof of its impact on marketing and business development. According to Invodo's publication of "Video Statistics for 2014", which is a compilation of leading research studies, shoppers who view video are 1.81x more likely to purchase than non-viewers. The retention rate for visual information can reach 65% vs. 10% for text-based information.

There are many telling statistics but here a just a few that illustrate how important video has become in the digital marketing world:

In December 2013, 188.2 million Americans watched 52.4 billion online videos; marking the first time the 50 billion video view mark was breached. 90% of consumers watch online video and 71% of consumers say that video is the best way to bring product features to life. It is estimated that 74% of all Internet traffic in 2017 will be video.

Clearly marketing professionals prefer video as their top choice for getting results in their marketing campaigns. The importance of using video to effectively convey your brand to your customer cannot be overly emphasized. Your customers are watching videos everyday on their computers or mobile devices. Have you implemented a strategy to reach this rapidly growing market?

Becoming a Good Digital Storyteller

"Marketing is no longer about the stuff that you make, but by the stories you tell." – Seth Godin

An effective video marketing campaign begins with a good story. Your audience is bombarded daily with lots of "digital noise". It is important to get their attention quickly since they only have so much time to spend. The objective is to get them from awareness of your product, service or brand to a higher level of intimacy where they form a trusting bond with what you are presenting.

Customer engagement is the new "Search Engine Optimization" so the goal is to get your audience to engage with you. There are many forms of engagement. For example, they could "like" your Facebook page, comment on a blog post, follow you on Twitter, attend one of your live webinars, join your membership site, or purchase your product or service. The best way to get your audience to respond the way you want them to is to become a good storyteller.

Storytelling is an effective strategy for marketing because we humans are wired to connect with each other. Stories make it easier for us to make those connections and form bridges with one another. Good marketing stories will resonate with your audience by invoking an emotional connection with the character(s) of the story. Behind each story is a meaning that your character is striving to convey, even if it is not specifically stated out loud.

Stories help people communicate and remember difficult ideas. Gustav Freytag (a famous 19th century German novelist) analyzed and developed a pictorial tool called the Freytag Pyramid, which illustrated the five common components of dramas. These five components are:

- **Exposition** – This is the scene where the story takes place and where the characters are introduced.

- **Inciting Incident** – Something happens that builds the anticipation of the conflict. Events occur, and you start to find clues.

- **Climax** – The conflict comes to a head.

- **Falling Action** – A reversal happens where the story begins to resolve. It's time to tell the reader more about why the character acted in a particular manner.

- **Resolution** – You reveal all the motivations and draw the story to a close.

Researchers have found that when we hear stories that utilize these components of a narrative pyramid, parts of our brain release endorphins (which are neurotransmitters that account for our emotions). When we connect with stories, we have an emotional response. It is that response which is needed in order to create relationships with others.

In business, you need compelling, truthful stories that will speak to your audience and accomplish the goals that you wish to achieve.

Here are the 6 Cs of Storytelling:

- **Connected** – Stories have to connect us to other people. They have to involve us in a shared experience.

- **Committed** – Storytelling is not a one-time event. Companies spent millions of dollars to reshape the way they engage and interact with audiences through content.

- **Customer** – The story has to have a character. The audience forms an emotional bond with that character. The characters you include have to be in conflict, and they have to have something to lose.

- **Crescendo** – The story has to have an ending. It needs to wrap up somehow. Don't leave an audience hanging.

- **Consistent** – Users interact digitally with each other on many devices every day. The story must remain available and consistent across all devices. The experience must maintain a consistent branding, style and tone throughout all channels.

In digital marketing, you make your story more compelling through video. Video generally serves one of two purposes:

1. **Video can support written content.** If you have a page of product information, you can use a video demonstration to support it and make it more impactful.

2. **Video replaces written content.** For example, you could get rid of your "About" page on your website and use a video to get people emotionally connected to your company and then use customer testimonials to provide social proof on how you helped that customer.

There are different types of videos that we detail in the next section, but they tend to have 4 basic flavors.

- **Branding** - Tends to be higher budget stuff and higher-production value.

- **Kinetic** - Words and images fly around the screen with a voiceover. They are meant to grab attention.

- **Product demonstration** - These videos are designed to be informative, educational, and inexpensive. They show people just like them using the product you are promoting.

- **Customer Testimonials** - As customers become brand advocates, they often can passionately tell your story on a more personal level than your employees.

10 Types of Videos

When you think of videos, you often think of a person (or multiple people) physically appearing on camera addressing an audience. However, effective videos often do not involve an on-camera appearance at all. In digital marketing, we have identified 10 primary types of videos that are typically produced.

1. **Direct to Camera** – This is the traditional type of video that is also referred to as a "talking head" video. In these videos, the subjects addresses their audience on camera by conveying information, ideas and stories and are highly effective in making an emotional connection with their audience.

2. **Webcast** – A webcast video utilizes various content delivery platforms such as Google Hangouts, YouTube Live, GoToWebinar and others to broadcast video to their audience in real time using a built-in or external webcam camera.

3. **PowerPoint to Video** – This type of video involves utilizing presentation software such as Microsoft PowerPoint or Apple Keynote to create a narrated slide presentation that is then turned into a video.

4. **Screencast** – A screencast video is created through a recording of your computer screen using available applications such as Tech Smith's Camtasia (Windows) or Telestream's Screenflow (MAC).

5. **Photo/Video Montage** – A montage can be created by adding photos and video clips and through animated motion, they can be turned into a video.

6. **Whiteboard or "Sketch" video** – This type of video utilizes simulated writing on a canvas or board that appears to sketch out the action on the screen. An example is a hand that holds a marker and appears to write out the words or draw out the characters that appear on the screen.

7. **Traditional Animation or Cartoon Video** – This is a video that utilizes animated characters and voice-over audio to tell a story or convey an idea to the viewer.

8. **Livecast (Online) Broadcast** – Similar to a webcast but usually more elaborate using a video camera and encoding

device to broadcast a live event. Often done with multiple cameras but can be a single camera as well.

9. **Interactive Video with Live Links or Annotation** – This video can involve both on-camera and screencast elements with links that appear within the video where viewers can click on to access external websites or content. For example, YouTube provides the ability to embed live links and annotations in the online videos.

10. **Interview Video with Two or More People on Camera** – These videos can be made by recording Skype interviews of people located in different places and turned into a recorded video showing the interviewees side-by-side on the screen.

Different Video Styles or Topics for Business

In the previous section, we identified 10 different types of videos that involve on-camera and off-camera techniques. There are also different video styles or topics that are used by business, which incorporate these different video types. These various styles are used to accomplish different objectives that you set forth for your specific videos.

Video Styles include:

1. The Welcome Video
2. The YouTube Video
3. The Squeeze Page Video
4. The Product Review Video

5. The Webinar Registration Video
6. The Thank You Video
7. The Sales Page Video
8. The Product Welcome Video
9. The About Me Video
10. The YouTube Trailer Video
11. The Book Trailer Video
12. The How to Teach Anything Template
13. The Upsell Video
14. The Stats Video
15. The Testimonial Video
16. The Interview Video (Virtual and Live)
17. The Tutorial Video
18. The Training Video
19. The Frequently Asked Questions Video (FAQs)
20. The Video Email

1. **The Welcome Video** – An example would be a welcome video on the homepage of your website. The video is intended to be an introduction to the content that the viewer will be accessing. Normally this would be a very short video – probably about a minute long and should be designed to motivate the viewer to access your posted content.

2. **The YouTube Video** – These are normally short videos that can convey a variety of messages and could be part of a blog for example.

3. **The Squeeze Page Video** – This video could be used to offer your viewers something of value in exchange for providing their contact information to you. For example, a squeeze page could offer a free whitepaper, free webinar or

training video in exchange for the viewer opting in to your page and providing their name and email address.

4. **The Product Review Video** – These videos are designed to provide feedback to viewers on a particular product or service. You often see these videos used to showcase new product introductions.

5. **The Webinar Registration Video** – This video would welcome and encourage viewers to register for your webinar event by explaining the benefits that the webinar content will provide them if they participate.

6. **The Thank You Video** – This video thanks the viewer for things like registering for your webinar, buying your product, or any other action that you requested from them, which they followed.

7. **The Sales Page Video** – This video explains all the benefits that the product you are selling provides and is designed to motivate them to want to purchase.

8. **The Product Welcome Video** – This video style is used to welcome your subscriber, or customer to the product they just purchased from you. It could include a roadmap on what to do next.

9. **The About Me Video** – This video can take the place of written text and offer the viewer a more personal introduction to yourself, your background and expertise. This approach is good to build trust between you and your potential customers.

10. **The YouTube Trailer Video** – Similar to a welcome video, this video is used to introduce viewers to the content on your YouTube channel.

11. **The Book Trailer Video** – This video is used to introduce your book to potential buyers and provide an introduction to the content of your book. It is designed to motivate the viewer to purchase your book.

12. **The How to Teach Anything Template** – These are videos designed to provide specific instruction on a given topic, whether it's building a physical item, learning a software application or a specific set of skills.

13. **The Upsell Video** – Once a prospect purchases a product from you, this type of video could be used to entice them to buy additional products immediately at the time of the initial purchase. Upsell videos are often used as part of a sales funnel campaign.

14. **The Stats Video** – These videos would provide the viewer with specific stats on a specific topic. For example, a video that talks about why you should use YouTube might include stats on how popular the site has become and compare the growth and use to other platforms.

15. **The Testimonial Video** – An important video is one that utilizes third party endorsements from customers or others who can provide social proof on why they may want to buy your product or hire you. This type of video is proven to be highly successful in developing a high level of trust and confidence between your potential customer and you.

16. **The Interview Video** – Often used in live or recorded events, these videos are between two or more individuals and are often in the form of questions and answers. A good type of video to use in a video podcast for example where a host or moderator might ask probing questions of a guest to educate their audience on a topic.

17. **The Tutorial Video** – An example of this type of video would be a software instructional course where the features of the software are shown and examples provided on how to create specific projects.

18. **The Training Video** – Similar to tutorial videos, these videos might be used in a company for example to show employees how to perform certain job tasks.

19. **The Frequently Asked Questions (FAQs) Video** – Videos can be created out of Q&A live webinars or events, which answer specific questions that are common to the customer. FAQ videos can also be used to reduce the demand on a company's support group by providing detailed instruction that the viewer can watch.

20. **The Video Email** – When video links are included in email messages, they tend to be more effective in engaging the customer. An email could include a graphic thumbnail in the email body and a link to access that video which is hosted on an external site.

Places to post your videos

Once you have created your video, you will need to determine where to post it to provide maximum exposure for your content.

YouTube, which is owned by Google, is the dominant player for video sharing but it is not the only site that you can utilize for posting your videos.

The results from a 2013 Online Video Marketing survey of 600 marketing professionals reveal that 94% of respondents utilize YouTube, 51% utilize Vimeo and 11% utilize Dailymotion. In addition, marketing professional use Facebook, Twitter and Linkedin most often for video sharing on social media sites. 87% indicated they post videos on Facebook, 70% on Twitter, 57% on Linkedin, 47% on Google+ and 24% on Pinterest.

What is important to note is that posting on multiple video sharing sites will provide the greatest exposure for your content and you shouldn't limit yourself to YouTube only.

Here are some of the most popular places that you can post your content (Not in any particular order).

1. YouTube
2. Vimeo
3. Facebook
4. Google+ account
5. Linkedin
6. Your Website
7. DailyMotion
8. Pinterest

9. Instagram
10. Tumblr
11. Slideshare.net
12. Twitter
13. Amazon S3 Account (for hosting video content)

You should carefully evaluate each hosting option to determine if it is right for you. In a later chapter we will be discussing how to measure success by looking at the various video metrics available on some of these video-sharing platforms, which help you gain an understanding on the effectiveness of your video.

Although YouTube is a the largest video sharing site, there are limited measurement tools available from YouTube, so you might benefit more by having your video on some of the other sharing sites that provide more comprehensive tools for measuring the success of your video.

Video Livecasting

In an earlier section we identified the different types of videos that you can create. One of the most effective types of videos you can do it referred to as livecasting (or live streaming video).

A livecast video is one in which the content is broadcast live over the Internet for people to access on any devices (e.g. smartphone, tablet, PC, Smart TV).

One of the questions that come up frequently is "Isn't it expensive to film a professional looking livecast video?" The answer may surprise you. With the tremendous technological advances in video streaming infrastructure made by companies such as Google, the ability to stream live video to literally thousands of people simultaneously is within the reach of just about everyone.

Not too long ago, to produce a good live video streaming event would have required equipment in the tens of thousands of dollars and expensive private transmission networks, but that is no longer true.

Today, there are easy to use platforms that you can utilize such as Google Hangouts or YouTube live to broadcast your content for free. Utilizing a decent webcam and a streaming network solution you could produce High Definition (HD) content on devices such as your smartphone, tablet, notebook or desktop computer.

When you publish or broadcast a livecast, you are leveraging the entire Internet to broadcast your content to anyone connected to the Internet, anywhere at anytime – for free. In addition to YouTube and Google, there are other companies that provide live streaming platforms at a low cost, including uStream.tv, Livestream.com and Justin.tv.

The equipment needed to produce a good livecast is inexpensive, ranging from the use of a simple webcam to the use of a consumer or pro video camera that you would equip with a video encoding device, such as those from Matrox, BlackMagic Design or LiveStream.   We would also recommend getting a decent microphone to make sure the audio comes across nice and clear. Depending on the content you want to produce, you can create and produce a good livecast for very little cost, or you can produce a higher end production for under $10,000.   Your smartphone and table can even be used to stream live content so the choices are plentiful and easy to deploy.

Google Hangouts have become very popular because they are easy to setup and free. You can use it to do webinars, interviews, panel discussions, video chats and webcasts. The Google Hangout can be any length and have unlimited attendees. It allows you also to have up to 10 other people on camera in the session and you are able to share your screen with the attendees. Hangouts can be set as private or you can do a "public" hangout.

The platform also includes an instant recording tool, which makes a recording of your broadcast for automatic posting to your YouTube channel.

Why would you want to do a Livecast video?

People love seeing video and there is no better way to engage your audience than by providing content geared specifically for them. A livecast helps you get your message out to the connected world and helps you build an audience and following that will result in new customer sales.

Here are some key benefits of Livecasts

1. Livecasts leverages available infrastructure to reach potentially thousands of people at the same time. Through services such as Google Hangouts, YouTube Live, Livestream and others, you can reach your audience with a minimal amount of technical skills needed.

2. The livecast gives you the opportunity to directly connect with your audience and establish credibility and trust through direct interaction. In addition, the live stream platform is accessible from any device, anywhere so it is simple for

people to login and participate in the event. Quite simply, people love watching a live event and are more likely to show up to be a part of the excitement.

3. Livecasts help create a buzz because you know that your audience is watching the live performance and they have the opportunity to directly interact with you. Knowing that it is all-live helps you better prepare your content and increases the excitement for all the participants.

Mike Koenigs, Chief Strategy Officer for The Pulse Network, has effectively mastered the use of livecasting to launch a number of information products. His livecasts have proved to be highly successful and have generated as much as $3.1 million dollars in one day. His last one grossed over $400,000 in a single day.

For Mike's livecasts, he invites customers to participate in the actual livecast to provide first hand testimonials of how the products he has produced transformed their own businesses. He also uses the livecast to talk about the features and benefits of the products, how they work and how they have helped his customers expend their businesses and make more money. Many of his livecasts draw hundreds or even thousands of prospects and customers who login to view part of the event. A chat box is used in the livecast to provide the viewers with the opportunity to ask questions and interact with one another.

In his particular experience, about half of the livecast attendees or viewers end up investing in the product.

An alternative to doing a live on-camera livecast, you can also do a live screencast where you are presenting content that you show from your computer screen. You could prepare a presentation using PowerPoint or Keynote, which is shown to your audience. You demonstrate a product or solution on the computer and engage in a Q&A with your audience.

Platforms like Google Hangouts provide the ability to share your screen with the attendees. Another popular provider for these type of broadcasts is Citrix's GoToMeeting (Webinar) which incorporates a number of tools that allow you to share your screen, or even change presenters to another user and have them share their screen.

There are added benefits from creating a livecast, such as recording the event and providing it to viewers who perhaps couldn't attend the live event. You can also break up the video into smaller chunks of content and use that in other marketing campaigns. Livecasts are a great way to build your business and set yourself apart from your competition.

Process of Creating Online Video Content

Now that you have a better understanding of what Video Marketing consists of and why it is so important if you want to build your business brand and get more customers, let's discuss the process of creating your online video content.

Step 1: Decide What Type of Video You Want to Create

There are a number of different types of videos you can make. In a prior section, we outlined the different video types and styles. You also need to decide whether the video will be an on-camera or off-camera variety.

Step 2: Determine the Objective for Your Video(s)

You will want to set the goals for the videos you are producing. What is the outcome you would like to achieve from these videos? What is the key message that you want to communicate to your audience?

Here are some possible goals you might want to achieve:

- Increase traffic to your company's website
- Develop and build your company's brand
- Grow your blog's subscribers
- Grow your YouTube Channel's subscribers
- Improve your user engagement
- Build inbound links to your website.
- Launch a new product or service

One of the most important factors in developing your objectives and goals is to determine the appropriate video content for optimizing the user experience. It is important to design and develop your content with the overall goal to encourage people to watch and respond to your videos.

Step 3: Storyboard Your Video and Develop Your Script

Video marketing industry expert Lou Bortone describes 5 Pillars of Video Marketing.

- **Purpose** – Write down your goals and objectives for the video. What do you need to accomplish?

- **Premise** – What is the key message that you want to communicate to your target market?

- **Platform** – How will you deliver the message? Will it be on-camera or off –camera? Will you include animation?

- **Promotion** – How will you share and distribute your video? Will you use social media, blogs, email and other promotional methods?

- **Profit** – How will you monetize and make money as a result of your video?

The process starts with picking your topic. You may wish to brainstorm some ideas. For example, you might ask: What's popular in mass media or in the news currently? What does our target audience find funny? What does our target audience want to learn about?

A common question that arises for many is "how do I develop my content for my videos?" One good approach that answers that question comes from Mike Koenigs (One of the most successful marketing entrepreneurs in the Country). Mike developed a system that addresses the challenge that many have as to what to talk about in their videos. He refers to this system as the 10x10x4 method. The 10x10x4 works like this:

Write down the **top ten frequently asked questions** (FAQs) you get about your product or service (this will only take about 15-30 minutes.).

Write down the top ten questions a potential buyer **SHOULD** be asking you about your product or service (SAQs). These are the important things that differentiate you from your competitors that you WISH they'd ask you (another short 15-30 minutes.)

Record 20 short videos responding to each question. Each video response should be 30 seconds to 2 minutes long.   [NOTE: You can do this as a 5x5x4 formula too, where you brainstorm 5 FAQs and 5 SAQs instead of 10 each.]

Now record the following 4 "mini" videos

1. The "**Call to Action**" Video. At the end of each video, you tell people where to go to get all your videos. You see, once you spread your 20 different videos all over the web, you'll offer people who viewed one of them the chance to see many more, all of them free—and to do that, they'll simply need to give you their name and email address.

2. The "**Enter your name and email to get all 20 videos**" video. Put this on your "lead capture page." It's your chance to connect with the visitor and explain your offer and why they should enter their contact information.

3. The "**Thank You for Signing Up**" video. Put this on your "Thank You" page—so when someone fills in the form, you tell them they'll receive their video as soon as they check their email.

4. The "**Buy My Stuff**" video. This is where you give the viewer an offer to either buy your product or service, or sign up for a consultation or trial.

Remember that your video is a sales message so you want to include the following when developing your script:

Start with a headline that grabs your audience's attention and offers them results.

For example, "In this video, I'll tell you how to break out of your rut, get your biggest dream off the ground, and build a life of your own design – without working 60 hours a week!"

Additional examples of other compelling headlines could include.

- "How to (desired result) without (downside) – How to triple your sales!
- "Do you make these mistakes?
- "What everybody ought to know about (blank)."

Keep your script outline short and focused and include:

- Headline
- Sub-Headline
- Bullet Points
- Call-to-Action

In addition to an attention-grabbing headline you will want to inject an emotional hook into your story and include yourself in the conversation. Vividly paint the problem that you are trying to solve and provide a solution. Most importantly be credible in your presentation.

Another aspect of storyboarding and scripting is to set out the details of your video script. For example, if your video will require multiple shots, characters and scenes you will want to script that out in detail and include set, stage actions and dialogue. If the video is conversational, you should create a list of bulleted notes that will help you stay organized during filming.

When writing out your script you will want to determine whether you will be using a teleprompter or not for the actual filming. For short videos, you might find it better to memorize your presentation or write out key bullets that you can cover in your video. For longer videos, you might find it better to utilize a teleprompter to make sure you convey your message exactly as you intend.

Be sure to write your script as you would say it in real life! Be conversational and natural in your approach. Most importantly, be yourself and genuine. You want to establish a strong connection with your audience and credibility is important.

Finally, your video should always have a call-to-action. What do you want people to do after they watch your video? Without a call-to-action your video will not meet your objective. We have seen many examples of videos that left the audience without any subsequent action to take and thus wasted the opportunity to further engage their audience.

The call-to-action should be strong and clear. You must tell your viewer exactly what you want them to do next! Some call-to-action examples include:

- Ask them to subscribe to your company's YouTube channel
- Complete an opt-in form to obtain additional free or paid content
- Friend your Facebook business page

- Follow you on Twitter
- Register for your free webinar
- Subscribe to your blog
- Visit a sales page to hear about special offers
- Buy your product or service offering

As you develop your content for your videos, keep in mind that you need to create high quality and compelling content. Most viewers will decide in the first few seconds of your video whether they'll keep watching. You need to retain their attention throughout the video but focus on making the beginning of your video captivating.

Creating good content addresses the needs of your targeted audience and answers the questions they are already asking. You should address what make your product or service unique and work to set yourself apart from other options they might be considering.

Finally, keep the video short. Less than 2 minutes is ideal and unless you are creating a full sales letter video, you should be able to effectively convey your message as quickly as possible and keep your audience engaged.

Step 4: Do you create your videos yourself or outsource?

One of the questions you will want to consider is whether you should create the videos yourself, or outsource part or all of the work. There are advantages and disadvantages to each approach, but you will want to ask yourself if you have the necessary skills, time and resources to film and edit the videos, or whether it would be better to find assistance in some of these areas of expertise.

It wasn't that long ago, that few individuals or companies would actually create their own video content because the equipment costs and expertise needed were so great that most didn't have qualified staff to perform this work.

However, extraordinary advances in video technology, along with corresponding declines in the cost of this technology makes it possible for many without a lot of training to create good quality videos at a low cost. Good videos can now be created on mobile devices such as iPhone and tablets with some basic training and low cost software tools that are available for these devices.

Of course, you can deploy higher end video hardware and software to achieve even higher quality but you can still create good, effective video content without breaking the bank.

More extensive productions can be made with the help of third party providers who created pieces of video content that can be inexpensively obtained through a variety of online sites and customized for your particular use.

Depending on the production quality needs of your videos, you might decide to acquire the necessary equipment and software to perform these tasks, or look for professionals who can provide these services to you. You will need to take stock of your own (or organization's) talents and resources to determine what is best for you.

In the next section we will discuss the type of equipment and resources you need to create high quality marketing videos.

Discussion of Hardware and Software for Video Creation

In this section, we will discuss the type of hardware, software and other resources you will need to create good, compelling marketing videos for your organization.

We generally do not discuss specific hardware or software products in this book, but do have a free video gear and resources guide available with our recommendations for specific equipment and software that you may wish to obtain. You can access the free guide by clicking on the link provided at the end of this chapter.

The **three key factors** that determine the quality of your video are: **Video Picture, Audio and Lighting**.

Potentially more critical than using a great camera, is using a quality microphone and minimizing extraneous background noise. Poor quality footage can still be a vessel for otherwise excellent content, but poor quality audio is more or less intolerable; meaning that while great visuals are valuable and useful in video, great audio recordings are more or less essential. Consider using lavalier microphones for interviews and vocal recordings where possible and investing in a reasonable quality camera Mic for capturing other audio in your scenes.

Shooting video with mobile devices:

The great technological advances of the past several years with mobile devices, such as smart phones and tablets have provided some unique opportunities to shoot video with devices that you might already own. Many of these devices will shoot high definition (1920x1080p) quality video. These video clips can be edited by available software on the mobile device, or the clips exported and imported to more robust video editing software.

One limitation of some of the video cameras on the mobile devices is the optical sensors tend not to capture good video in low light settings. You will need to make sure you have adequate lighting available when shooting your video. Another important consideration is utilizing an external microphone to capture audio such as a lavalier or a hand-held microphone. You do not want to use the built in microphones from these devices since you will not get the results you need to produce a high quality video.

You will also want to get a tripod and mount that you can use with your mobile device. Another popular accessory is a "selfie stick" which is a telescopic pole that has a mount on the end, which you can use to extend your camera out several feet to take video of yourself and others.

Recommended Equipment:

- iPhone or Android phone with built in HD quality video camera
- External microphone (Lavalier or hand-held microphone)
- Tripod and mount for an iPhone or tablet
- External lighting if shooting in low-light environments.
- Collapsible (telescopic) selfie stick
- Video editing software

Mini Studio Setup:

Many marketing videos are shot with a white or other background to provide more versatility in post production to add graphics to the screen. You may wish to setup a mini studio where you can achieve a wider variety of video styles and effects. You can setup a good quality studio for under $4,000.

Video Equipment:

You will need a video camera (camcorder with HD quality video and an external Mic input is recommended). Minimum required features in the video camera should include good low light video capture, white balance capability, optical and digital zooming.

You can also use a DSLR (Digital Single Lens Reflex) camera with video capabilities. There are a number of cameras on the market that shoot both still photos and video. Keep in mind that many DSLRs will only shoot short video clips (around 8 minutes or so) at a time. Because of the versatility of settings within a DSLR, they are quite popular as a video capture device.

Tripod:

You should have a good full-size tripod for mounting the camcorder or DSLR. We would recommend a tripod that has a visual leveler on it so you can insure the camera is level. You might want to also have a tripod with a fluid head if you want to do any panning during the video shoot.

It might be handy to have multiple tripods if for example you want to place a tripod on a desk or other service. You can get smaller tripods for these types of situations.

Audio:

As mentioned earlier, you do not want to use the built-in microphone on the video camera since you will get a hallow (tin-can) sounding audio output if you are filming a subject not next to the camera. The built-in audio is also not very good at reducing extraneous noise from the environment around you.

You will want to get a good Mic or variety of Mics that will plug in to your video equipment. For interviews or single subject videos, you could use a lavalier Mic (Mic that connects to your lapel area). Lavalier Mics are either wired or wireless depending on your needs (and budget).

Other Mics include a handheld Mic (for interviews) and general-purpose use, or a shotgun Mic which is a directional Mic that is usually mounted on a portable pole that will capture audio in a scene. The use of a shotgun Mic is nice if you don't want to have the Mic visibly in the scene.

Another option is to use a portable audio recorder (sometimes referred to as a field recorder), which can capture audio that is later synced to the video in post-production.

Lighting Options:

You will want to acquire some good lighting to provide even lighting of your subject and background. Not long ago, lighting usually required very hot tungsten lights, which consumed a lot of power and produced unwanted heat. Fortunately, advanced in LED and fluorescent lights have made tungsten lights nearly obsolete. LED and fluorescent lights use very little electricity and throw off virtually no heat. They have become very popular for video studio setups.

Fluorescent lights are generally less expensive but advances in LED technology have continued to lower the cost of LED lights. We would recommend getting daylight temperature lights for your studio (Usually around 5,000 to 5,600 degree Kelvin). Sometimes these are referred to as cool lights (versus warm lights which cast a softer (yellower) hue). Further discussion on lighting configuration can be found in the chapter on lighting consideration.

Teleprompter:

If you are going to shoot a number of videos and think you will need a teleprompter there are some good low cost solutions out there. Some of these solutions utilize an iPad or other tablet in conjunction with a hardware box that creates the teleprompter functionality. Inexpensive teleprompter apps are available to load and run your content on your tablet and just like that you have a great teleprompting option.

Backdrop:

If you want to shoot in front of a backdrop (for example, white, black, green or other color), you can acquire a video backdrop kit, which are usually two stands and a crossbar for hanging the backdrop. An inexpensive backdrop solution is to get continuous roll paper (such as white or other color), which can be mounted on the crossbar and rolled down to create your desired backdrop. Green screen shots often used a green muslin material.

Video Editing Software:

Once you shoot your videos, you will want to edit them using a video editing software package on either a MAC or PC computer. We will discuss this further in the section on video editing.

Summary of Recommended Equipment:

- Video Camcorder or DSLR camera with video capability
- External headphones to monitor the audio output from your video camera
- Tripod (full-size and portable for desktop)
- External Mic(s) – Lavalier, handheld or shotgun
- Lighting kit (to light the subject and backdrop if required)
- Teleprompter (hardware for using iPad or other tablet)
- Backdrop stands and backdrop material (paper roll or muslin backdrop)
- Video editing software

Remember, there are lots of options out there to shoot good videos and you don't need to spend a fortune to have a professional setup for your video shoots. Mobile devices are a good way to shoot quick videos – particularly outdoors.

Recording your Videos

Once you have acquired the necessary equipment to create your videos, and have scripted out your content, the next step is to record the video itself.

Here are some tips to follow when recording your video content:

1. Find a suitable location – You will need to find a place that has very few distractions. Consider issues such as background noise (e.g. traffic, construction equipment etc.). If indoors, consider the size of the area, available lighting, overly bright windows, and equipment or people noise that might interfere with your filming.

2. If outdoors, consider the lighting conditions of the area in which you want to shoot. Watch for unwanted shadows from trees, structures or other objects. Also, if there is any wind you will need to have a wind screen for your microphone to damper the noise from the wind.

3. It is always best if you have an assistant to help you with the filming (could be a friend or spouse). Give yourself enough time to do the setup and takedown and to do multiple takes that will likely be required to get the shots you desire.

4. Make sure you have access to electrical power if you need to plug anything in. For battery-powered equipment, it may be best to have extra batteries on hand.

5. Always shoot some test takes and review them before doing the actual filming to check the audio, lighting and video output to make sure it is working as desired.

We mentioned previously that the 3 key factors that determine the quality of your video are Video Picture, Audio and Lighting. Here are some common mistakes that you should avoid:

- **Bad Audio** – Usually because you are too far away from the camera or microphone, or not using a windscreen when recording outdoors with breezy or windy conditions. Always check your audio input levels and monitor the audio with headphones.

- **Poor Lighting** – Not enough, or too much light on your subject. Light coming from behind the subject instead of in front of the subject. Shadows stemming from improper lighting setup or from objects around the shot location (if outdoors).

- **Bad Framing** - The shot is setup with the subject too far away from the camera, or too much headroom in the shot. Adhere to the rule of thirds when framing. Divide the background and subject into thirds and make sure they are set evenly within these parameters.

- **Too Long** – The content is too long. The subject begins to ramble.

- **Bad background** – The background of your video is too busy, cluttered or distracting. Also, don't use a window as a backdrop if too much light is coming through. This tends to make the subject too dark in the foreground.

1. Set the Scene for Your Video:

A) Before filming, first "set your stage". Details are critically important! If you are using a tripod, make sure it's level. Are their papers or unnecessary objects in the scene?   Are there any classified or confidential information in the background that should be removed?

B) Make sure your scenes stay consistent – known as maintaining continuity. For example, if there is a cup or object in the scene in the first take, make sure it is still there in subsequent takes.

2. Utilize Specific Camera Shots and Filming Techniques

To make your content more interesting and more professional looking, think about the best angle and perspective for your shot.

1. **Over Shoulder:** Shooting over the shoulder of your subject to show the perspective of one person listening to another person.

2. **Low Angle Shot:** Shooting at a camera angle by putting the camera below an individual, pointing up. This gives the person on the camera an essence of power and strength. This is good for presidential figures, bosses and heroes.

3. **High-Angle Shot:** The opposite of the low angle shot. Shooting from a vantage above the subject looking down at them makes the character seem timid, lost or young. This works well if you want to show an adult looking down at a child or a superior looking down at a frightened employee about to be reprimanded.

4. **Bust Shot:** Good for video interviews. Frame your subject from the belly button up, or lap if they are sitting. Make sure you frame it so that you can see hand gestures and

interaction.

5. **Close Up:** This shot shows detail of a character's face and focuses on their expression. A good shot to use if your subject is displaying a strong emotion or has an epiphany.

You may also want to vary your shots by taking multiple shots from multiple perspectives. However, maintain the 180-degree rule, which is important to not confuse the viewer by seeing the subject appearing from different directions in the same scene.

3. Recording Quality Audio

We cannot overly emphasize how important it is to have high-quality audio in your video production. It has been shown through research that viewers are much more forgiving of video quality than they are of poor audio. People need to clearly hear the dialog to understand what's going on.

Here is a checklist to ensure quality audio:

1. Use a set of noise-cancelling headphones, which you will plug into your camera to listen to the audio feel while you are recording. By doing this, you will hear any unwanted background noise, static or other unwanted audio issues.

2. Always conduct a sound check before you start recording. Check the audio level and sound quality.

3. Remove all background noises if possible. Check for buzzing noises stemming from refrigerators, ventilation system or office lighting.

4. Avoid filming in open rooms with tile or other building materials that could create echoes. You could place blankets or other sound damping objects around your filming area to reduce these issues if necessary.

5. Make sure you pause or stop recording if you detect loud noises during the filming, such as construction, sirens, doors slamming etc.

Use the proper microphone for the scene. If an interview, you can use individual lavalier Mics to individually Mic each person in your video. You could also use a shotgun (boom) Mic to capture the audio in a scene if the subjects are close to one another. Wireless Mics are great if you want to avoid dealing with the wires that need to be concealed, or if your subjects are too far from the camera to effectively use wireless Mics, or if they need to move about in a scene.

4. Lighting Considerations

Good lighting is an important factor in creating good video quality. Whether it's natural light for outdoor shooting, or indoor lighting in a studio, obtaining and deploying the correct lighting configuration can make the difference between great content and poor content.

When shooting an indoor studio environment, you will want to setup a 3 point lighting configuration – Key light, fill light and a back or hair light.

- The key light is the primary light facing the person being shot.
- The fill light is slightly to the right or left of the person, and

fills the area with light.

- The backlight is directly above and behind the subject. It removes shadows and gives the person's hair a nice glow and really makes them pop out from the background.

You want to avoid recording a scene with a window in the background since the bright light will make your subject dark. You also want to avoid creating shadows as much as possible so the lights should be positioned to create an even light across the subject(s). Too much light can wash out the people in the video so adjusting the intensity and distance of the light from the subject will help create the proper balance.

Backdrop Lighting

If you are planning on using a backdrop for your video shoots, you will probably want to light the background as well, especially if you are wanting to shoot pure white background videos. The key is to have enough lighting shining on the background to create an overexpose in your camera; and that's how you get that nice pure white effect (popular in many videos and commercials). Also, if you plan on shooting green screen videos you will want to make sure to get a nice even light on the backdrop.

Lighting - Color Temperature

White lights are rated by color temperature from cool to warm. Cool lights actually have a higher Kelvin temperature (around 5,000 to 6,000 Kelvin) and approximate outdoor natural daylight color. Warm lights have a lower Kelvin temperature (2,000 to 3,500 Kelvin) and take on a more yellow/orangish tint.

Most video cameras have the ability to set the white balance to make sure that the camera adjusts for the different temperature colors to avoid unintended hues in the video picture. What you don't want to do is mix different light temperatures because it is difficult to do proper white balancing.

When shooting indoors, you should be aware of the office lighting. Most office fluorescent lights are in the lower Kelvin temperature range (warm) and therefore if you add cool lights to your set you might want to shut off the regular office lighting when shooting your videos.

LED or Fluorescent?

As mentioned previously videographers used hot tungsten lights for many years, but fortunately advances in lighting technology over the past several years has pretty much done away with tungsten lighting. We would literally see our tungsten lights smoke with the intense heat coming of these so we welcome these new lighting types.

Fluorescent lights come in many configurations and Kelvin light temperatures. You can get cool or warm fluorescent light panels for your lighting and they use much less electricity and throw off very little heat. The downside is that you can't dim these lights and they are somewhat bulky to work with. The price point of these lights is pretty competitive and represents a good cost effective solution.

LED lights are rapidly becoming the standard that many videographers are adopting. Prices have been declining over the last few years and although they are still more expensive than fluorescent lights, they can be set to dim, use very little electricity and throw off no heat. In addition, they are pretty durable and have a long life for the LEDs.

If your budget allows, we would recommend LED lights since they are quickly becoming the industry standard.

For more information on recommended video hardware, audio, light kits and other resources, you can click on the link at the end of this chapter for our free gear and resource guide.

The Video Editing Process

Once you have filmed your raw video footage you will likely need to do some editing of the videos to use for your desired purpose. It is in the editing process were magic is created and your story and message comes to life. Editing is a detail-oriented process where small changes can have a big impact on the final video product.

Fortunately, the software to perform the editing continues to get better and easier to use. Without a great deal of experience, users can perform basic editing tasks and quickly produce some very good videos. However, with some added instruction, users can learn some nifty tips for making their videos really shine.

This is a good spot for discussing whether video editing should be done in-house or outsourced?

Taking video footage and turning it into effective videos for marketing is an art that does require some knowledge, skills and imagination. It is possible to do some basic editing for the novice but if you really want to produce high quality videos, particularly if you want to add graphics and other content to the final videos, you will want to either have someone in-house with some experience in video editing techniques, or look to outsource the video editing work.

There are many good sources to outsource the editing, much of which can be found at sites on the Internet. A quick shameless plug for the authors of this book who can provide assistance in video editing, training and guide you to additional outsource resources where you can turn your video into a higher quality product.

Quick Guide to the Editing Process:

1. Video Editing Tools

There are many good video editing tools available, ranging from simple apps on your smartphone and tablet to more extensive software editing programs that run on the Apple MAC or PC Windows platforms.

Here are some of the more popular applications:

<u>Basic editing applications</u>

- **IMovie** – This is an Apple product that comes free on all MAC computers and IOS devices. It's a nice drag-and-drop style tool that will do easy, yet professional-quality videos. IMovie exports files as .mov format, which can be uploaded to most video sharing sites.

- **Windows Movie Maker** – Free Microsoft product with features that are similar to iMovie. Video files are exported as .wmv files.

Intermediate/Pro Video Editors

- **Techsmith's Camtasia** – Camtasia is great for creating screencasts (recordings of your desktop) and provides some fairly robust editing capability. The application supports multiple video exporting options to most of the popular formats. You can also import in regular video footage to be integrated with the screencasts so it is a complete editor solution. This application is designed to run on a Windows environment.

- **Telestream's Screenflow** – This is an editing program similar to Camtasia but designed to run on a MAC computer. With Screenflow you can also create screencasts and import video files with some pretty good editing tools. Files can be exported in multiple formats.

- **Adobe Premier CC 2014** – This is a more advanced video-editing platform with many tools to create good videos. Multiple export formats supported. It is cross platform for MAC and Windows.

- **Apple Final Cut** – This is a popular and robust video editing application, which runs on the Apple MAC. It also is feature rich and supports multiple export formats.

- **Sony Vegas Pro** – Another very robust video editing platform which will run on a MAC or Windows platform.

- **AVID Promedia Composer** – Advanced film editor with similar features to Final Cut. Cross platform compatible.

Unless you are a professional video editor, we recommend staying with solutions such as Camtasia or Screenflow which provide good editing capabilities at a reasonable price, without a steep learning curve.

Which is better for video editing – PC or a MAC?

This is a question that is often asked and the answer really comes down to personal preference and quite honestly the user's experience with one platform or the other.

Apple MAC's have traditionally been popular with video editors because of the available software and operating system that performs well for video and graphics. However, PCs running Windows also have a number of good video editing software platforms available so you can't really go wrong with either choice.

<u>The Editing Process</u>

Regardless of which video editing software you choose, most of them work on the premise that video clips are imported as assets to a project and then placed on a timeline where you can perform various edits and add additional graphics, annotations and other elements to your video.

There are both basic edit and advanced edits that you can perform on your video clips. Basic edits include cuts, transitions and trims. Advanced edits include adding graphics, lower-thirds and music to your video. If you were filming in front of a green screen, advanced editing would also include chroma key (removing the green background and replacing it with an alternative background.

One key tip for working with any video-editing project is to use an external hard drive for storing your video files. Raw video files from your camera can be quite large and if you are working with a number of projects, you can quickly fill up your drive with these clips.

The general editing process for all video projects is:

1. Create a new video project in your software application
2. Import your video clips into your project
3. Choose which clips you want to use for your video
4. Edit these clips together, make trims and utilize transitions where desired
5. Add any additional graphics and music if desired
6. Export the completed project to your desired format.

The most challenging part of editing is determining which clips and parts of clips to use and throwing away the rest. Remember, you want to keep your videos short and to the point so only use what gets your message across most effectively.

Here are a few tips when editing your clips together. You will want to use a transition at the beginning and end of your video. A good beginning transition is a fade-in and a close with a fade-out. Usually a one second fade in and out will work well. Fade-ins and fade-outs can also work when depicting the end of one scene and the beginning on a new one.

Some other transitions you may want to use in your videos include a "cut transition" and "dissolve". A cut is a quick edit between video clips where one immediately cuts to the next without a transition. A dissolve is a gradual transition between clips where you see the new clip appear as the old one ends.

Some additional advanced editing techniques include adding graphics to your video, such as annotations, lower-thirds (used to display titles of the person on the video), clip art, photos etc. One advantage of shooting video against a bright white background is you create a canvas in which to place these graphics. There are many resources available where you can obtain graphics, stock footage, animations, illustrations and other content to spruce up your videos. Make sure you click on the link at the end of the chapter to get our resource guide, which lists some of these resources that you can access.

Another good addition to your videos is adding music to the background. Music can be a great way of enhancing the effectiveness of your videos by setting a specific mood in a scene. Can you imagine watching a motion picture movie without the accompanying music used often throughout the film?

If you do add music, remember to only incorporate music that you have royalty-free rights to use. Never use copyrighted music in your videos. Video sharing sites such as YouTube will remove your video if it detects the presence of copywritten music. Worse yet, you could get sued. There are many sources for music that you can inexpensively acquire to use in your videos, which provide you with royalty-free use. Our resource guide provides some of these resource locations.

Exporting your Completed Videos

Once you are content with the completed edited video, you will want to export that video into a format to be uploaded to the location you will use for posting your video content. Most of the video editing software tools will export your video for you in a format that can be used to upload to the video sharing sites. One of the most popular formats today is an .mp4 file. This format will work in virtually all the video sharing sites and is supported by PCs, MACs, IOS devices (iPhones, iPads) and Android devices.

When exporting HD quality videos, we recommend using the original resolution of 1920 x 1080 (1080p), or 1280 x 720 (720p).

Distribution of your Videos

Now that you have created, edited and finalized your video, it is time to introduce it to your target audience. In an earlier section, we provided a list of the top video sharing sites where you will want to publish your video. However, publishing the video is only the first step. You will also need to promote your video to draw people to your content and then provide a method of engagement through a call-to-action.

Where you publish your video should align with the original goals that you established for the video itself. You should utilize the popular video sharing sites, such as YouTube and Vimeo, but you can also decide to self host your videos on a third party server, such as Amazon S3 and then utilize links back to your site or landing pages to promote the videos. Placing your videos on YouTube and Vimeo will result in more exposure for your video since these sites also serve as a search engine where metatags for your video content are indexed and searchable.

Publishing your Video on YouTube, or Other Video Sharing Sites

YouTube is the largest video sharing site in the world with more than 1 billion unique users visiting their site each month. Over 6 billion hours of video are watched each month on YouTube.

Since YouTube is the 2nd largest search engine in the world, publishing your videos to their site gives you the opportunity of having your videos indexed and the content accessible by anyone in the world who can access that site. Best of all, publishing your videos to YouTube is Free.

If you haven't already done so, you will want to setup your YouTube Account and setup your YouTube Channel. There are many tutorials available to walk you through that process, but it is fairly straightforward.

A few suggestions that you will want to keep in mind: First of all, you should create a banner header graphic for your YouTube channel which you will be able to upload and display when users access your YouTube site. On the banner header, you will be able to add a clickable link such as your website URL address.

You will also want to consider creating a "Welcome to your YouTube Channel" video which users can watch when they visit your YouTube site. Make sure you have added a description of your channel so viewers can learn more about your business and have the ability to click back to your website.

When posting your individual videos on your YouTube site, you can create playlists and also add titles and tags to your videos to make them easier to find. It is always very important to add a URL link back to your website in the description for each video.

Within the videos itself, YouTube allows you to add annotations on your videos so that users can click on a link while viewing the video which can take them back to your website, landing page or other location. Make sure you always have some form of call-to-action in your video so viewers know what you want them to do next after viewing the video.

When you publish your videos to YouTube you will be able to grab the embed code, or share link from your video and place that on your website page, landing page, or other site. By embedding the link, you will be providing the viewer with the ability to access the video right from your website or other location without having to actually go to your YouTube channel to watch the video.

In addition to YouTube, you can also choose to post your videos on other popular video sharing sites such as Vimeo where you will also be able to set up a free account and upload your videos.

In addition to the main video sharing sites, here are some of the other places you might consider sharing your content:

- Your Web pages
- Your Blog
- Email Campaigns
- Your Partner blogs
- Press Releases
- Email Campaigns
- Facebook
- Twitter

- Linkedin
- Google+
- Instagram
- Pinterest
- SlideShare

Bonus Material: we will provide more specific details on how to setup and use the popular video sharing sites in our **Digital Marketing Mastery membership portal** that you can access. <u>A free trial membership is included when you purchased this book and register on our site.</u>

Video Promotion Campaign

After you have uploaded your videos, the next step is to develop a campaign to promote your videos. This campaign should be multi-faceted with the goal of driving viewers to your website, landing pages or to take additional action that you specify in your videos.

Specifically, you are aiming to attract prospects to your marketing funnel and collect contact information. You are seeking to qualify your leads as they work their way through the funnel and drive them to the next desired action. For your most engaged prospects, you will develop more specific, targeted messaging to convert them to actual customers.

According to Vidyard (Video Analytical Platform provider) "In today's digital buying landscape, the customer journey usually begins with search." According to the Demand Gen Report, 81% of B2B buyers start their process with a general web search. In just so happens that video is one of the best ways of getting your content to rank on the results pages of search engines. According to Forrester, pages with Video are 50x more likely to rank on the first page.

Vidyard goes on to state that "overall, you can generate demand at the top of the funnel with high-level how-to videos you release on YouTube, as well as entertaining content you host on your site. The key to your top-of-funnel videos is to remember they should always point back to your website where prospects face fewer distractions, more of your owned media, and more opportunities to enter the funnel and, eventually, convert."

By strategically placing your content on various sharing sites and through specific targeted campaigns, you will drive prospects to your website, or campaign landing page

Website or Campaign Landing Page

Approximately 70% of the buying process is completed independently before buyers ever talk to sales. That is why it is important that you offer informational and guided product tours on your site to educate your prospects. Videos embedded on your site can help increase conversion by 80% (Vidyard). Moreover, Google tracks and recognizes pages where users spend more time viewing leading to higher page rankings in Google Search.

Email Campaigns

A GetResponse study found that out of nearly one billion emails, those containing video had a 96% higher click-through rate compared to non-video emails.

Incorporating videos in your emails (usually through links and thumbnails) you will achieve far more success in your campaigns.

Social Networks

We have already discussed the importance of posting your videos to the main video sharing sites, but it is also important to utilize the other social networks in your promotional campaigns.

Posting your content in Facebook, Twitter, Linkedin, Google+, as well as others such as Instagram and Pinterest is part of an integrated strategy that will help drive traffic to your campaigns.

We will cover in more detail the use of social media to promote your business and videos in a subsequent chapter. The overall goal here is to create an integrated campaign that will get your content in front of as many people as possible so you can build your list of prospects that convert at a high rate to actual customers.

With any of the promotional strategies, you will find that the **most important thing that you need to do to add sales to your bottom line is to tell the viewer what to do next after watching your video.** You must prompt them to perform a marketing-related action (e.g. download a white paper, start a free trial, schedule a demo, register for a webinar, watch another video etc.).

While your audience is engaged with your content, you will want to include a clear call-to-action to direct your viewer what to do next. Perhaps the call-to-action is to watch another video that starts them on a journey through your sales funnel. You could even have a series of videos that provides a product tour, which leads to a purchase opportunity.

Remember that when creating your call-to-actions, be specific with your language (e.g. Click to start your free trial today!). Always use the proper wording to convey a sense of urgency and keep the viewers on a specific path that leads them through the buying process.

Measuring the Success of your Video Promotion

Once you have created your videos, uploaded the content, and implemented your promotional campaigns, you will want to measure the success. The question then becomes, how do you measure success? The answer depends on the objectives that you set forth.

If driving traffic to your website was your objective, than you might want to analyze how many people viewed your video and then type your company's URL into their browser. You could also look at the search traffic your website received for your company name to see if that increased the week after launching your video.

If your goal was to extend your social media reach, you might want to measure the growth of subscribers to your blog and YouTube Channel. With more subscribers, you can touch more people when promoting new content in the future.

One of the most important goals is probably related to dollars in the bank (The Bottom Line!). Did your video result in more customer engagement that directly leads to more sales? Sometimes, it is difficult to gauge the impact of your video and separate that impact from other aspects of your marketing campaign. It is here that gaining an understanding of the key metrics of your video marketing campaign will be most important.

With the rapid adoption of video as a strategy to build customer engagement, the industry is turning to results measurements as one of the most important tools to gauge the success of your campaigns. By analyzing the data on how your video is performing you will be able to determine whether that video is delivering the return on investment that you expected.

Here are some of the key metrics you should evaluating:

Please note that not all of these metrics are available on standard video sharing sites.

- Number of views for your video
- Average amount of time that the viewers are watching your video.
- Number of viewers that watch the video to completion
- Average time in the video that viewers stop watching (exit) your video
- Number of videos in a marketing funnel that the viewer watches
- Number of page views to the landing page
- Increase in comments on your Blog page
- Click-through rate
- Number of opt-ins on your landing page
- Conversion rate
- Number of inbound links
- Number of social shares
- Overall site rankings
- Overall sales
- Difference in key metrics from A/B Testing

Number of views for your video?

How many times is your video viewed and over what period of time (i.e. – hours, days etc.).

Average amount of time that the viewers are watching your video?

More useful than total number of views, this key metric measures how much of the video on average your viewers are watching.

Number of viewers that watch the video to completion?

Of the number of unique viewers of your video, how many of them are watching the video in its entirety?

Average time in the video that viewers stop watching (exit) your video?

At what point in your video is the average viewer leaving your video? If your video is 4 minutes long for example and the average exit point in the video is at 30 seconds, you may need to reevaluate the message and length in the video since most viewers are not watching the majority of the video.

Number of videos in a marketing funnel that the viewer watches?

If you have a series of videos in your marketing funnel, it would be helpful to monitor how many of these videos your prospect is actually viewing.

Number of page views to the landing page?

You could look at the total number of page views that your video landing page is receiving to see how effective your campaign is in driving traffic to that page.

Increase in comments on your Blog page?

If you are driving traffic to a video on your Blog site, you could monitor how many additional comments you are getting to see how engaged your audience is in the content that you posted.

Click-through rate?

How many times are viewers clicking on the links provided in your video, landing page, or email? You would measure the number of click-throughs compared to the total number of times the video was viewed.

Number of Opt-ins on your landing page?

How many times are viewers opting in to a campaign on your landing page?

Conversion rate?

Of the viewers who click on your links and opt-in, how many of them are ultimately taking the action you requested (purchasing, downloading, registering etc.)?

Number of inbound links?

There are methods available to determine how many external links have been created to access your video, or landing page.

Number of social shares?

When posting on Facebook, Twitter, Linkedin, etc., how many times are people sharing these posts with others on these sites?

Overall site rankings?

What is the page ranking of your landing page as determined by Google or other search engines?

Overall sales?

What are the sales created through the campaign you have launched?

Difference in key metrics from A/B Testing?

A popular strategy is to do testing of the same video with different tags, description, key words etc. to determine which posting is most effective. The same could be done with the wording on your landing page to determine how the key metrics change from one version to the other.

Summary of Key Points to the Video Marketing Strategy:

- *Recognize the importance of video marketing as a key tool in your arsenal.*
- *The use of videos leads to higher conversion rates.*
- *Learn how to become a good digital storyteller.*
- *Select the type of video you want to produce.*
- *Understand how the different video topics or styles are used to accomplish your objectives.*
- *Know where the best places are to post your videos.*
- *Utilize video livecasting to effectively reach your audience.*
- *Recognize the process on how to create online video content.*
- *The hardware and software that is needed to create effective videos.*
- *How to properly record your videos.*
- *Video editing is where the magic is created.*
- *The strategies on publishing and promoting your video content.*
- *The tools to analyze the results of your video campaign.*

BECOME VIDEO PROFICIENT – GET YOUR FREE BONUS CONTENT?

Register for the FREE book updates, training videos, livecasts, video gear guide and access to our Digital Marketing Mastery Training Portal.

Visit http://0s4.com/r/MRK3B4 or
(Http://www.riseabovethecloud.net) or
text **Bookbonus** to 58885 or
text your email address to 1-805-601-8001

STRATEGY 2: MOBILE MARKETING

"The majority of internet usage will be done via a mobile device and for most people the mobile web will be their primary, if not their only, way of experiencing the internet. " – Peter Rojas (Gizmodo)

In 2014, we saw a continued uptick in the number of consumers using mobile devices like smartphones and tablets. Consumers used them to research and compare products and make deals, often right in the store. Many analysts and experts predict that 2015 will be an even bigger year for mobile, with people not only researching and comparing products on their mobile devices but purchasing them from their smartphones and tablets as well.

As a marketing pro, when thinking about how to incorporate mobile elements into a comprehensive marketing strategy, you must not assume "Mobile Marketing" is similar to your other marketing efforts. While there is a similarity in concept, utilizing mobile applications is truly unique.

Creating a marketing strategy that targets consumers with relevant products to purchase while they are in a retail location makes mobile marketing a viable answer. It makes it more relevant and less intrusive. In addition, social media networks, accessed on mobile devices, will be a main channel for real-time location based marketing, providing the key advertising platforms for businesses looking to target customers with location based offers.

"You must not assume "Mobile Marketing" is similar to your other marketing efforts"

Of course, communications that are accessed on mobile devices are also available on Internet sites, including the social media channels you access from your office or home computer. However, if you want to be effective with mobile marketing, you must think of it as a medium unto itself.

You will need to consider such factors as; how personal people consider their devices. Remember that in addition to carrying around their iPads or Tablets, most people have their cell phones or smartphones with them 24/7 365 days of the year. You can't get more personal than that.

Another factor to consider is how your customers or prospects will respond to the marketing program you have launched considering that they will have to opt into your campaign. Keep in mind, where your customers or prospects are located geographically is also a factor in trying to reach out to them effectively in the mobile world. With this in mind, it is our hope that the information the authors provide in this book will help you to rise above the "Cloud" and become a leader in mobile marketing.

"Optimizing content," is usually associated with "Search Engine Optimization" and creating "relevant keywords." Today, when it comes to the world of digital marketing, there are many other factors that have a wider influential impact in optimizing content. There are many who operate in the digital world that will tell you that "Trust and Credibility" are more important than "content alone".

However, please keep in mind that trust and credibility does not displace content because you can only build trust through reliable content. While mobile marketing strategies have proven to be effective, they are also much less expensive than traditional means of advertising. Interesting enough, the strategies employed are simple enough for any age group to understand and employ.

Planning your Mobile Strategy

There are certain things that you need to think about before you consider creating the right mobile strategy. Planning in advance is critical. Will you want to create a program to generate email lists for the purpose of compiling sales leads or newsletter subscribers? What is your goal? What would you like to achieve? Obviously, you must know the target market that you are trying to attract so that you stay focused on your objective.

Through the years it has been our experience that helped us to learn that every successful business that stood out above their competition had something special going for them; some hook or angle that drove more customers to them rather than to their competition.

"Trust and Credibility" are more important than "Content alone"

Do you have an angle or a feature that could be more attractive or inspiring to the target market you are pursuing? If not, consider a unique way to share your information between various mobile devices or have people who communicate through the Web, share the information you created and posted.

You must distribute your creative content on a regular basis by releasing updates in order to maintain continued interest. This can be accomplished through regular video webinars and assisted by various, "Auto-responding" software that is readily available. It is also important to understand how well your content is being received by effectively tracking, analyzing and optimizing it.

How effective has mobile marketing been? Currently, you can see mobile marketing advertising being done on a variety of smartphones and tablets. The general consensus is that mobile marketing is very effective. While their styles may vary, each platform is unique in how the ads might display. Today, utilizing mobile marketing is as important as having Wi-Fi on your computer. Wherever you go these days you will see people everywhere glaring down on their smartphones.

2014 was the most successful year in e-commerce sales and one of the first times we saw mobile contribute a significant amount to overall spending growth. This was particularly true during the 2014 holiday season, as mobile traffic accounted for 45% of all online traffic from November-December. Amazon reported that more than half of their customers used mobile devices to shop over the holidays, while large brick and mortar retailer Wal-Mart exceeded 84% over the past year. Wal-Mart also saw more than 70% of web traffic come from mobile devices between Thanksgiving and Cyber Monday in 2014.

Analysts predict that the trend will continue as consumers reduce desktop and in-store purchases, especially as mobile devices become easier to shop on and retailers put more dollars behind mobile strategies.

"Today, utilizing mobile marketing is as important as having Wi-Fi on your computer"

There have been recent reports that show nearly 35 to 40 percent of individuals that utilize the Web are spending more time on a variety of available mobile products. By not using or embracing this new mobile marketing technology your marketing strategy will be at a distinct disadvantage. It can also be safely assumed that glancing over a myriad amount of data on mobile devices is a tactic that is here to stay. If projections have any validity, mobile devices will soon be eclipsing the customary desktop usage.

When it comes to businesses, under the right circumstances, their name and "Brands" can be substantially rewarded. When the right conditions are in place and your mobile marketing campaign is done correctly, you will be able reach the customers in your market by way of a mobile message that your customers, while they might yet not know it, will actually want to hear. However, do not engage in marketing activities that might be labeled "Spam". Mobile marketing is not sending out volumes' of unwanted content and text messages via cell phone to individuals or business who most likely will not want, have any need for, or have no relation or business relativity with the business sending out the messages.

Although the Mobile Marketing Association defines mobile marketing as: "a set of practices that enables organizations to communicate and engage with their audience in an interactive and relevant manner through any mobile device or network", it is important to note that businesses communicating with consumers on their mobile devices should only do so with permission or an "opt-in" agreement in advance. The content being sent must be timely and relevant to your customer's business or service.

Today, the average consumer can receive or request text messages on their cell phones when they are out shopping, at home watching TV or reading a book. Consumers can also use their mobile devices to find your business or mobile website. They can also call your business spontaneously wherever they are. Customers can also use their smartphones to find out their location and use that information to request coupons from nearby businesses or find a local restaurant of their choosing. In that regard, mobile devices will most likely become so involved in people's daily lives that living without them will become unimaginable. Responding directly to advertising on mobile devices is a quick and easy process.

The majority of those who use mobile devices have the device with them at all times, even while they're driving or walking down the street. If they forget their phone at home, people will return home to pick up their device.

The goal of a successful mobile marketing campaign is getting your customer to interact with you. Because of the mobile technology, your customer can and will interact with you. However, first you must create a mobile marketing campaign that will compel your customers or new prospects to want to interact with you and your business.

"Mobile devices will most likely become so involved in people's daily lives that living without them will become unimaginable"

Many people engaged in mobile marketing mistakenly believe mobile marketing is similar or a smaller version of the Internet or television. Of course, this is not the case. In reality, the Mobile industry is both unique and massive as a medium. Of course this is true for the industries that cater to the print, audio recording, radio, cinema, TV, and the Internet. While mobile has become the newest medium for consumers, it has become the most widespread worldwide.

Mobile is different than the Internet because consumers interact with the mobile web differently. For one thing, mobile devices utilize a smaller interface then on a regular full-size computer. As a result, consumers by and large don't browse on mobile as they are usually in a hurry and seeking information quickly or in some cases, using the device for entertainment.

Consumers purposely use mobile devices when they are not in the same frame of mind as they are when using their desktop browsers. It is important to keep in mind that when creating an effective mobile marketing campaign that your content must be specifically focused on the subject matter that they "opted-in" for. Also, consumers are unimpressed when they find a version of your content on their mobile devices that is diluted. This results in having your content being received as being useless. Always be prepared to give your consumers as much content as possible regardless of what mobile platform is being used. Make it easy for users to find exactly what they need in a few clicks as possible. One click would be perfect.

Welcome to the Smartphone

When the iPhone was introduced in 2007, it made a huge impact on mobile marketing. Its initial use in North America was embraced immediately. Currently, there are numerous manufacturers of smartphones, which include android phones, blackberries, and others.

All these new phones continue to have an impact on mobile marketing. Already accounting for the bulk of mobile-phone sales in the U.S., smartphones accounted for 55 percent of all new cellphone subscriptions globally, up from just 40 percent a year ago according to a new report from Ericsson. Smartphones have become a factor on how quickly mobile marketing is being accepted and expanding.

Since the current group of mobile devices has a broader range of functionality, consumers are finding themselves doing more with them and connecting with businesses in more interactive ways. Utilizing mobile apps and mobile websites, consumers now have the ability to pay for most products and services.

Marketing with Mobile Business Apps

If you were thinking that mobile apps are strictly for big name brands like Wal-Mart and Bank of America, you would be wrong. More and more small and midsize businesses are following the mobile trend, understanding that an effective mobile strategy involves more than just a mobile-friendly website.

There are approximately 30 million small businesses in the United States alone. While it is estimated that 91 % of those businesses do not have a mobile presence, that is changing quickly as more small businesses are beginning to adapt to the new technology. You probably have already seen a mobile app being available for your local neighborhood restaurant, retail shop or hair salon.

For the longest time, coffee shops and carwashes and all manner of businesses have handed out buy-10-get-one-free punch cards with a hope to reap the rewards of this simplest of loyalty marketing campaigns. With the inception of mobile apps, a new day has arrived. Now, local businesses, who have a business app use the features on the app to stay in touch with their customers through notifying them of varying specials discounts or, in the case of restaurants, "weekend 2 for 1 " dinner or luncheon specials. Mobile apps are rapidly becoming an extremely effective marketing tool.

According to the data provided by the University of Alabama at Birmingham's Online Masters in Management Information Systems, by the end of 2015, 1 billion smartphones will have been sold; twice as many as the number of personal computers. At the present time, the average mobile app user spends more than 30 hours a month on over 24 different apps. The data showed 46% of app users paid for their apps. By 2017, it is predicted that over 268 billion downloads will generate $77 billion worth of revenue. This segment of the mobile industry is showing no signs of slowing down.

Customers are paying for apps more and more, instead of just opting for the free versions. According to the research:

- 46% of app users report they have paid for an app.
- 52% say the highest they have paid for an app is $5 or less.
- 17% have paid more than $20 for an app.
- Of the people most likely to pay for apps, are men, Adults aged 30 and older college graduates, Adults with an income of $50,000 or more, and those living in urban cities.
- Revenue for apps is expected to grow from the current $11.4 billion, to $24.5 billion by 2016; that is a 400% increase.

By the end of 2015, 1 in 3 consumer brands will feature integrated payment in their mobile apps. By 2017, 48% of revenues will be from in-app purchases particularly with the introduction of "Apple Pay" which is now incorporated into the iPhone 6 models.

Broken down by age group, the statistics are as follows:

- Of 18-24 year olds, users averaged around 28 apps per month, spending 37 hours, and six minutes per month.
- Of 25-34 year olds, users averaged 29.5 apps per month, spending 35 hours and 40 minutes per month.

By 2016, the world's population will be approximately 7.3 billion. 91% of the U.S. population will own a cell phone, and of these, 61% will be smartphone users. 1,000,000,000 cell phones will be sold that year, double the number of PCs expected to sell.

With more and more people acquiring smartphones every day, and more people relying heavily on apps for every day needs and wants, it only makes sense for any business to consider utilizing a customized business app as part of their marketing strategy.

Features Available on Mobile Apps

Contact/Social Features
- Around Us: Highlight businesses or locations with a specialized map view displaying points of interest.
- Call Us: Easy, one-touch calling.
- Contact: Combined call, email, and directions capabilities, plus social integration and more!
- Direction View: One-touch directions.
- Email Form: Customizable email submission forms.
- Email Photo: Quick photo send tool.
- Fan Wall: Comment board for customers & fans alike.
- Mailing List: Easy subscription-building feature.
- Messages: Push notification log.

- Social: Facebook, Twitter & Google+ integration, plus quick stats on user engagement.
- WuFoo Form: Direct integration for highly customizable email submission forms.

Entertainment Features

- Image Gallery: Add custom galleries or link up your Instagram, Flickr, or Picasa account.
- Music: Upload mp3s or link to iTunes & 7Digital tracks.
- News: Display relevant, keyword-based content from Google News, Facebook & Twitter.
- Podcast: Integrate your podcast right into the app.
- RSS Feed: Pull in your RSS feed for in-app viewing.
- YouTube Channel: Feature your YouTube channel video stream.

Practical Features

- Car Finder: Never lose track of where you parked with this timer-based solution.
- Info: Display great, customizable content with our 3-tiered tabs.
- Membership: Limit access to your app with password-protection.
- Mortgage Calculator: Quick tool to add up what you'll be paying.
- Notepad: Jot down anything you need to remember on this built-in pad.
- PDF: Upload or link to PDFs for easy in-app display.
- QR Scanner: Built-in QR scanner for quick use.
- Sports Stats: Track scores in-app.
- Tip Calculator: Make sure your users aren't under tipping

your servers.

- Voice Recording: Record & email audio.
- Walkthrough: Great intro tool to onboard new users and highlight key features.
- Web Site: Simple URL tool that allows you to integrate any site.

Mobile Apps Can Integrate With:

- Facebook
- Twitter
- Google+
- YouTube
- WuFoo
- PayPal
- Google Maps
- Google News
- Flickr
- Picasa
- Instagram

- iContact
- Constant Contact
- Campaign Monitor
- GetResponse
- Emma
- Volusion
- Magento
- Shopify
- iTunes
- 7Digi

Here are seven major benefits for incorporating a mobile app as part of a mobile marketing strategy:

- Visibility to your customers or clients at all times
- Create a direct marketing channel to your customers or clients
- Provide value to your customers or clients
- Build brand recognition
- Improve customer or client engagement
- Stand out from your competitors
- Cultivate customer or client loyalty

The "loyalty" factor is extremely important but is at risk when you consider how your customers or clients are subjected to the vast area of marketing media via roadside banners, billboards, flashing signs, newspaper ads, flyers, coupons, websites, website banners, Facebook ads and email marketing. Incorporating a mobile app as part of your strategy could help by being a way for your customers or clients staying closer to you since they are just a "fingertip" away at all times.

Smartphones with a loyalty app feature have begun offering small businesses enhanced features that offer the same advantages of automated administration capabilities once affordable only to large companies like airlines and hotel chains. These capabilities also offer the equivalent of a real-world psychology lab for easily evaluating the effects of offerings and incentives on customer loyalty. As an example, as people get closer to having a completed card, the time between visits gets smaller."

Smartphones that can pinpoint a user's location may provide additional marketing opportunities to people who've downloaded loyalty apps. A mobile technology developed by Apple, iBeacon, allows businesses to know if a regular customer is near their storefront and ping them — or even greet them by name as they cross the threshold.

Professor Urminsky of the University of Chicago said a strategy built on mobile apps to reward loyalty — in essence, "a loyalty platform rather than an isolated loyalty program" — opens new possibilities for small businesses. "If it's used wisely," he said, "I think it will be a game changer."

The fact is, the more powerful these mobile devices become, the more businesses will incorporate mobile marketing as part of their business strategy.

In addition to Smartphones, tablet sales are enjoying explosive growth now. Tablet shipments are forecast to average a *CAGR of 24 percent over the period 2012-2017, rising from 2012 shipments of 136 million, to 2013 shipments of 208 million, going on to 2017 shipments of 398 million devices. Due to this rapid growth in smartphone and tablet sales, they forecast that over the period 2012-2017, the number of apps users will grow at a CAGR of 29.8 percent, to reach 4.4 billion users by the end of 2017, 4 times as many apps users as there are today. *Compound average growth rate*

The Ever Expanding Mobile Market Place

The mobile market place continues to expand each year. Currently, there are more than 5 billion active cell phone subscribers, which represent more than 73% of the World's population. Mobile users represent a huge market. The next time you are out and about in a public place, just look around you and see how many people are on their mobile devices. They are most likely making calls, searching online, sending text messages or checking their email.

It is amazing when you compare this to the number of people who, may be reading newspapers or magazines, or who might be listening to the radio or watching television. Mobile devices have become the mass media of choice when it comes to individual connectivity. However, just because the number of mobile users has grown and is continuing to grow in record numbers, does not mean they are receptive to marketing campaigns directed to their personal mobile devices.

"Utilizing mobile apps and mobile websites, consumers now have the ability to pay for most products and services"

It just means that an opportunity exists for you to reach your customers much easier and with a personal touch. Of course, at the same time, your customers will also be able to reach you easier than ever as well. Because of the sheer number of users who have access to mobile devices, the growth of advertisers who are taking advantage of this media continues to grow. By 2009, during a very depressed economy, mobile advertising revenue grew 85% from 3.1 billion to 5.9 billion. By contrast, according to "Fiksu" mobile advertising data, in 2014, mobile advertising generated around $18 billion. Mobile apps were a big part of that.

It is important to know that having a successful website is based on your ability to convert people successfully from a site visitor to an opt-in person on your SMS or email list. If you have millions of visitors to your site that don't connect with you in some way, then your site will be useless.

You may not think this is important if you are only selling advertising based on the traffic you are receiving. However, if your advertisers don't get the exposure they are expecting, they will not return. This could spell failure for your site.

On the other hand, if you are retail store and offer your location, hours, and other information to your site visitors, there is still the possibility of a conversion that might result by getting these mobile web visitors to physically visit your place of business. Make sure you get your visitors to take some type of action while they are on your site.

The Importance of Having a "Call to Action"

Be sure that your call to action is a prominent feature on your mobile site. If you want people to sign up for text messaging, or any other type of information you are offering, it is extremely important that you add your code to the "call to action" segment on the site. If you plan to build an email list, make sure your email "opt-in" box is in a location that can be easily seen. If you are selling any type of products or services on your mobile site, make sure the order process is simple and convenient. It is also important that you add your "call to action" link on every page on the site.

If you want your visitors to opt into a text message campaign from your mobile website, what value or incentive are you willing to offer? If you are offering something free, be sure to explain all the benefits they will receive. Try to make it compelling enough so that they will opt-in allowing for a higher conversion rate. However, if you don't provide enough value for your visitors, they will not opt-in and your conversion will decrease.

Of course, you may not think you are ready to launch a mobile campaign. However, your customers might already be reviewing content on your web site by way of their cell phones. Your customers are currently using their mobile devices to interact on their social media networks. As a result, they may stumble upon your company's name or website on their mobile devices.

Whether you are using mobile or not, in reality, your business is already interacting with customers in the mobile environment. If you fail to pay attention, or ignore what's happening, you will run the risk of losing out to your competition who, may have already begun to launch their mobile marketing campaigns.

An effective mobile marketing campaign is different than conventional marketing programs in that your customers must be actively involved in the marketing in order to get started. This is later discussed in more depth in our "Social Media" chapter.

Once your campaign gets started, your business, through your marketing efforts, becomes an indirect one-to-one relationship with your customers. For example, when your text message is sent to their phones, it will most likely be read immediately. Your mobile website should offer the right diversity of content so your customers can immediately recognize your business right on their mobile devices.

Creating an effective marketing campaign does not just suddenly happen. Time has to be spent doing strategic planning to make sure the campaign works the way you planned it and that it achieves a direct customer connection.

Your marketing campaign should have lots of vitality to it. It should be energetic and full of enthusiasm with a strong sense of purpose. It is important that you create a campaign that has a defined objective. Only if your campaign works smoothly between you and your customers will you have an effective, timely and profitable campaign.

With respect to the basics of marketing, there are two ways to reach customers.

- The first is to aggressively initiate your marketing to them. Or essentially, push marketing in an effort to actively reach out to your target market without getting their prior permission or even if they have no interest in receiving your messages as far as you know. This kind of aggressive marketing is seen in the use of commercials that interrupt shows on television or music on the radio or sending unsolicited sales oriented emails or text messages. Most individuals have a distinct aversion to this type of marketing because, unless there is some prior interest, no one wants to have messages or ads pushed at them, especially when they are not interested in any of the products or services that are being offered.

"It is important that you create a campaign that has a defined objective"

- The other way is to attract or pull customers to you. Marketing that draws customers usually contains content that your target market will actually want to receive. By sending this kind of content directly to them, you are able to market your company to them as well.

This type of strategy will often find customers forgetting where the content is coming from because they are enjoying the benefits derived from what they have received.

If the marketing campaign you designed is based upon carefully attracting customers, by doing it properly, customers will ask you for your content. All that needs to be done is put the content or offer in front of your customers repeatedly.

It is recommended that attracting customers with a well-planned marketing strategy might include building an effective website and inviting your customers to check it out and:

- Creating a newsletter and encouraging customers to sign up for it.

- Producing a video that shows viewers how to do something.

- Offering potential customers in a value such as a discount or timely information in exchange for permission to send them a text message.

It is interesting that, under certain circumstances, both types of marketing methods will work. Aggressive marketing thrust upon consumers has worked for hundreds of years. If it didn't, countries around the world would no longer be using this option. A perfect example is pre-approved credit cards finding their way into your mailbox.

Attracting Customers or Clients with Content

The smartest and most effective marketing strategy is to attract customers first with content that will entice them to "Opt-in" for future marketing messages that will be sent to them on a frequent basis and on topics that they are interested in. Not only is this smart marketing, it is the perfect strategy to support SMS text messaging.

The fact is, the era of mass merchandising is ending. The marketing world has changed and while mass tactics that work so brilliantly 35 - 40 years before, which is understanding given the media available at that time, needs to be re-evaluated in this new era of mobile technology and instant communication worldwide.

People don't like to be receiving information related to a marketing campaign when they feel like they are being coerced into buying something. But while individuals like adding something of value to their lives, or when they feel that they are receiving something that is enhancing their lives, they are willing to be directly involved.

> *"A brand is no longer what we tell a consumer what it is. It is what consumers tell each other what it is" - Scott Cook*

It is interesting to note that when customers are exposed to something that is really worthwhile or something they really want, they do not feel like they are being subjected to a marketing pitch. There are many examples of this like, receiving software or computer updates, or receiving opportunities for product discounts from reliable or familiar consumer sources.

Having previously "opted in" to these vendors, customers can verify the source of the text message when it arrives and since the message has "Relevant Value", the feeling of "being marketed to" becomes a non-factor.

Knowing what your customers want and what you are willing to provide to them is an important part of creating your mobile marketing campaign. Here is a following list of questions that you might want to ask:

- What information do you think your customers need from you and, would need right now?

- What do you think the most common questions your customers ask?

- Is there any knowledge about your products, services, or

business history that your customers would find interesting or helpful?

- What do you think your customers would like to receive in the way of bonus material or services you offer as a reward prize?

- Do you or, will you allow your customers to offer their opinions or insights on specific topics?

- Do you sell a product or service that your customers can buy quickly or impulsively?

- Can you compile a list of questions and answers about your company, or the products or services you offer?

- What information alerts about day–to–day operations do you think your customers would want or need?

- Does your company sell products for which a video tutorial would be useful?

- Do you exhibit any trade shows?

- What fundraising efforts do you do?

- Where can potential customers see you or your product? An event? Workshop? Seminar?

- What new products or services do you have that your customers can be the first to know about, buy, use, or experience?

- What kinds of coupons would be useful to your customers?

- Do you sponsor any events that your customers attend?

The answer to these questions will be helpful in designing your marketing campaign. Once you begin to incorporate the technology part of your campaign, it will allow you to concentrate on what you will be offering your customers. Adding relevant, valued content to your customer's lives through your mobile marketing campaigns will allow you to be successful in the first step of designing effective mobile marketing campaigns.

Attracting new customers is probably the most important marketing objective of any business. Most advertising created is designed for that marketing purpose. Yet, marketers often find that it is easier to increase sales from existing customers by keeping them happy than it is to keep trying to attract new customers.

Since mobile applications are such an interactive tool when combined with other marketing efforts, it is easier to market a campaign with a proven strategy that is aimed at current customers.

Who to Contact First

As an agenda, we first suggest that you concentrate your marketing attention on increasing your sales to current customers. Then, when you feel more comfortable with your mobile marketing results, move to the real and more important objective of acquiring new customers.

It is possible to achieve a positive outcome with mobile marketing as long as you are providing excellent and timely content that has value to your target market.

Because your existing customers are already buying from you, it is easier to generate more sales to them. Since they have already been receiving your other marketing pieces, they trust you.

As you plan your marketing strategy, mobile will be an essential part in increasing your sales from this key market. Be sure to offer financial incentives to current customers as well as new ones. Don't just offer your best deals to new customers. Be sure to offer your best deals to your existing customer base as well as it will prevent your customers from resenting you and moving their business elsewhere.

Keeping your existing customers is predicated upon providing good customer service. This can be accomplished by creating a friendly, mobile responsive website with emails or text messages that can be easily read on a variety of mobile devices.

It should be easy for your customers to interact with you. This could be in the form of an inquiry message to you or, a product or service that they would like to order from you. Regardless of what, responding in a timely manner will help to retain your customers.

The most important objective of any business, new or old, is how to attract new customers. While it involves creating a different kind of strategy because new customers are not a part of your current sphere of influence, accomplishing this objective is exciting and will pay vast dividends for your efforts. However, remember when you are trying to attract new customers, your marketing efforts and mobile campaigns must be different from your regular in store marketing efforts to ensure you are attracting new customers and not just current ones.

"The most important objective of any business, new or old, is how to attract new customers"

Effective Methods to Get New Customers or Clients

While there are several conventional ways to attract new customers or clients, Mike Paule, founder and President of MobileData360 and co-Author of this book, has created a video that describes a special marketing campaign that is designed to effectively and quickly attract new customers and generate new profit streams (http://www.mobilevideo360.com/videos)

Here is a list of activities that will help you to develop a plan of action as you undertake your mobile marketing campaign.

- Make sure your current business is fully mobile capable.
- Make your website mobile friendly and see that all your data and emails can be read on all mobile devices.
- Maximize your mobile marketing by selecting the strategies that best fit your business.
- Create an SMS text messaging campaign.
- Create a QR code to allow your print advertising to become mobile responsive.
- Develop your mobile SEO capabilities.
- Create an effective mobile advertising campaign.
- Be sure to include click to call incorporated into each application or strategy you develop.
- Actively and aggressively market your mobile campaigns.

- Be sure to include using social networking to promote your mobile campaigns.

There are many reasons why Mobile Marketers should never send unsolicited messages to individual's phones. One of the primary reasons is the 2003, US CAN- SPAM Act. This law applies to email and to commercial text messaging on SMTP servers that send unsolicited messages to cell phones.

Though at this time the CAN-SPAM Act only applies to the category of mobile marketing, there is legislation being discussed at the state and federal level, which might include provisions that are more stringent.

As a result, it would be wise to follow the law when using an SMTP messaging service because sooner or later it will apply to all other forms of text messaging. In addition, In the US, it is against the law to buy or rent lists of mobile phone numbers and then send text messages to these phone numbers. Even if you should send email or text messages that your customers have requested, you need to remain observant of the legal guidelines.

In addition, there are more important requirements that specifically apply to mobile messaging. As an example, you must offer a way for customers to "opt-out" on receiving your email messages, While sending mobile messages to individuals should have prior "opt- in" permission, there must be a provision in your message that allow the recipient of your email to "opt-out" of any further solicitation.

In other words, mobile marketers are legally required to get prior authorization before sending any commercial messages to a mobile device while, also offering a way for customers to stop receiving messages.

It is important that you receive prior authorization orally or in writing before marketing a mobile campaign to a new customers list. This can be accomplished in several ways:

The first way, and usually the best way, is a mobile opt-in. This means the customer sends a text to your pre-prepared request code. Another way is to have your customer fill out a form on your website and then send either a pin number or an opt-in message to your phone. With prior permission, you can also use one of your staff members to manually enter a customer's name into your opt-in customer list.

Upon completion, your customer will receive a confirmation message. It is very important to follow the required steps so that you have an exact record that prior permission was granted.

Once customers have opted in to your marketing campaign, it will now be safe to send them text messages in reply to their requests and, or other messages specifically related to your campaign. However, you should not be sending any other information that is not related to the campaign they opted in for. (*For more information we suggest reading from the "Mobile Marketing Association Consumer Best Practices Guidelines" at www.mmaglobal.com/bestpractices*).

Summary of Key Points to the Mobile Marketing Strategy

- *Participate in the rapid growth of the mobile marketing trend.*
- *Target consumers with relevant products or services to purchase.*
- *Understand consumers' use of mobile devices in their day-to-day- activities.*
- *Utilize opt-in strategies.*
- *Effectively Plan your mobile marketing strategies.*
- *Incorporate the strategy of using mobile business apps.*
- *Utilize customer loyalty programs in your mobile app.*
- *Create an effective call-to-action in your mobile campaigns.*
- *Use SMS Text messaging to effectively communicate to your audience.*
- *Create compelling content to engage your customers and prospects.*
- *Make sure your business has a fully responsive mobile optimized website.*

MAKE MOBILE MARKETING WORK FOR YOU!

Register for the FREE book updates, training videos, livecasts, video gear guide and access to our Digital Marketing Mastery Training Portal.

Visit http://0s4.com/r/MRK3B4 or
(Http://www.riseabovethecloud.net) or
text **Bookbonus** to 58885 or
text your email address to 1-805-601-8001

STRATEGY 3: PUBLISHING YOUR BOOK FOR CREDIBILITY AND PROFIT

"Nothing is so powerful as an idea whose time has come" - Victor Hugo

In 2007 Steve Jobs, the founder and CEO of Apple Computers revolutionized "Smartphone" technology, which prior had already been previously gaining ground in the business community. He introduced the "iPhone" to the world. It was a game-changing event.

Because of Its numerous advance features, in both ergonomically as well as functionality, it ushered in the beginning of several industries that today represent billions of dollars. It is amazing that this all occurred in just 8 short years! Today the Mobile Phone industry consists of 10 different operating systems; the 2 major ones being Apple's iOS and Android's operating system.

This new technology also set the foundation for what is known as the "Tablet" led by the introduction of Apple's iPad. These new products have fostered new opportunities in the area of business, marketing, education, and music including a vast array of other professional and personal categories of interest.

One of the categories that have grown as a result is the area of self-publishing. Did you know it is now possible to write, produce, publish, distribute, and make money with your idea all for <u>free</u>! It's true!

Depending upon your content and the audience you are appealing to, with some strong and well-planned marketing efforts, you can become a well-known and respected expert in your field! Even a celebrity!

Here is an overview of how to profit from writing and publishing your book. The first thing you will want to do is to prepare by planning what subject or subjects you want to write about? Who and where is the audience that you want to focus on? What name or title will you give your book? Will it have sub-titles? Do you have a special angle or hook in your story?

"It is now possible to write, produce, publish, distribute, and make money with your idea ...all for free!"

We realize this can be a little overwhelming when you start so a little later on we have prepared an outline that lays out a series of steps that can guide you through the process. In the meantime, what would be a reason for you to even contemplate writing a book? Well, some of the reasons might be to make money, sell a product, build a customer list, enhance your personal credibility, and convey a special message or life-long passion.

In asking this question to entrepreneurs that we interview, we have found that the majority of whom we speak to, say that they want to make money and share their message. In that regard, "How to make money and convey a message" will be the focus of our discussion in this segment of our book.

Once you have decided upon the subject matter for your book and the audience that it is intended for, you can begin to perform your content. This can be done easily by answering questions, interviewing other specialists in their field or just telling stories. While this seems very simplistic, this technique is very effective and can be used for creating other media like video, audios, books or other products.

The Advantages of Performing Your Book

Performing the content as suggested is an alternative to locking yourself in a room and tediously typing your ideas on your computer. Hello "writer's block"! As mentioned earlier, we will discuss our step-by-step approach to organizing this technique.

The whole objective here is to publish your book and have it be read anywhere, everywhere or at any time. The good news is Google, Apple and Amazon will publish your book and pay you 70% for your content at the same time promoting and marketing your book to the world while making sure it can be seen, heard and read on any internet-connected device.

You can have an audio version of your book or it could be turned into a special course or training materials on your subject matter. The incredible thing about all this is that your access to publishing, marketing and promoting your book through these multi-billion dollar companies is free!

In addition to having your book available as an "E-Book", able to be downloaded electronically, you can also take advantage of having a version of your book produced as a 'Paperback" by using the services of "Print on Demand". Of course, there are fees associated with this service but the good news is that you can control your costs because you only need to actually produce as many copies as you want; from one to thousands!

Where will your audience come from? According to recent reports, right now there are almost 3 billion smartphones in use word-wide. There are 3 billion internet-connected desktop and laptop computers including approximately 2 billion internet-connected tablets, which include iPads, Androids and Kindle devices, which are currently outselling computers.

Consider hundreds of millions of people drive their car to and from work every day of which, according to Arbitron, 39% of them are listening to streaming audio or Podcasts. Of course you also have to throw in nearly 300 million internet-connected televisions including Smart TVs and Apple TVs.

By targeting your marketing efforts to this incredible and vast body of consumers You will be able to leverage the advantage of having free distribution with partners that virtually have unlimited shelf space. The purchase of your book by an interested consumer is as simple as a single click on any of their mobile devices.

The Advantages of Being a Published Author

As a published author, it creates a conversational environment with people who may be prospects; it encourages new relationships that help to build trust. Almost instantly you can be in the pockets of every mobile device user; selling products, services or even getting paid for just recommending somebody else's products or services through a myriad of affiliate relationships. Although a subject that we will discuss in more detail a little later, you will need to inspire, motivate and persuade your audience to do business with you. One place to start is utilizing the social media sites, which are <u>free</u>.

According to a study by Pew Research, 73% of the human race is involved with some aspect of social media. That equates to a universe of 5.1 billion people at your disposal. This is why you have to take advantage of the <u>free</u> social distribution channels available on Google, YouTube, Apple, Amazon, Facebook, Linkedin and other social sites in order to have the world read, watch or listen to your content.

"Almost instantly you can be in the pockets of every
mobile device user"

Creating an audio version of your book can educate and inspire your listeners and readers while it helps to build a trusting relationship with them. The interesting thing about the content of your book is that it can be re-formatted and released and translated into any language, allowing you to reach out to the vast global market.

Your book now becomes the centerpiece of creating social media content, written articles and material for radio, television, speeches and both video and audio podcasts.

Congratulations! You are now a best-selling author with a new kind of credibility and recognition. New clients are seeking you out regularly! This all happened because, you followed a system that helped you to prepare your book, select a title and, create a great story with an interesting angle.

The method that you used was to perform the content in your book creating questions and answers, telling stories and interviewing experts in the field of your subject matter. Upon completion, you published the content in your book utilizing several of the largest distribution companies in the world like Amazon, Apple and Google so that you your book could be seen, heard and read everywhere. Finally, you promoted your book on every social site in the world reaching out to nearly 5.1 billion people!

Making Money with Your Book

Now comes the most important part, making money with your book. Once it gains momentum, you will want to create a business around it that pays you every month with a stream of passive income that will give you the kind of independence that you deserve.

Part of this process comes at the conclusion of each chapter in your book, which should include a call-to-action ("CTA"). Since one of your marketing objectives is to build a customer list, you will want to, at some point, communicate directly with your readers in order to monetize your efforts as a published author.

In order to establish that relationship you will need to harvest your reader's email address by offering valued information relative to the content in your book, for free. It could be a free trial membership to a service, a special video or audio that they could download on other materials that you had previously produced relative to the content in your book or other related products that are produced by others in which you have an affiliated relationship.

The book is your starting point. It is your way to get your foot in the door and by-pass the people who stand in front and who are an impediment to reaching the people who are the real decision-makers. The content in your book discusses the "What" issues and problems contained in your subject matter which should ideally drive your reader to the "How" or products and services that address the issues that are being discussed. It's the products and services that you sell where the real money is rather than the royalties that you might earn from your book.

If you already have a product or a service to offer your book will give you more exposure, credibility, authority and celebrity value which can offer you a buffer against your competition.

There are quite a few reasons for this. Other than earning royalties and publishing advances, as a published author on a particular subject, it will be easier to create a community among an audience that have similar interests. Your book will also allow you a voice in the social media. As you build your audience list, your celebrity value will help you participate in speaking events as well as promote special live events.

Your book and other collateral materials regarding your subject can be used as giveaways at trade shows. Your book and the celebrity value it created can help with new product launches. In addition to getting paid consulting assignments, your book can also be promoted during teleseminars, webinars and livecasts. These are but a few ideas limited by your own imagination.

"It's the products and services that you sell where the real money is rather than the royalties that you might earn from your book"

According to best-selling author, Mike Koenigs, writing a book is more about psychology then technology. It's about mindset over matter. Once you understand the difference between the "what" and "how" as mentioned previously, some of the answers begin to flow naturally. Other basic questions that need to be asked is "who" is my book for and "why" will they buy my book? Also, "how" will I grow my list of prospects and customers and make money with my book and build my business?

The answer to "why" is that your book will give you and your business instant credibility. There is something about being a published author that seems to make people treat you differently. Unlike a business card, they don't throw away your book. Your book shows everybody how smart you are and is written proof of your knowledge and wisdom and experience without coming off as braggart. It creates a certain celebrity status that can change the dynamics of who you are and how you are being perceived, especially when someone introduces you and mentions that you are a published author on a given subject.

Your book can run interference for you because for only a few dollars you can mail it to a prospect in order to get your foot in the door and past those people who stand in the way of the decision makers you want to contact.

"It creates a certain celebrity status that can change the dynamics of who you are and how you are being perceived"

You can actually buy your books on Amazon, have them gift wrapped and sent to your prospects and receive your royalty check from Amazon for your effort! I would rather doubt that your prospect would ignore receiving a personal gift-wrapped package from Amazon or, for that matter, allow their secretary or assistant to open it on their behalf.

When a prospect receives and reads your book it basically tells them whom you are and in a sense, creates a one-way conversation that tells them what you do, how you think and most importantly, provides the reason why they should do business

Using Your Book as a Lead Generator

Another advantage being a published author is to help generate leads and build your list of customers.   As all successful marketers will say, getting new customers and keeping them is the most critical aspect to developing a business with solid staying power.   It is an ongoing, continues effort involving both mining and processing.

Each chapter in your book should be designed to tell a story filled with information that answers questions and shows that you care and that you know what you are talking about and are prepared to solve whatever challenges that your reader may be confronted with.

Throughout your book, especially at the conclusion of each chapter, you will insert a "call-to-action" section that will invite your reader to visit a specially designed opt-in web page to enter their contact information in order to receive some sort of bonus material or a gift. As mentioned earlier, it could include training videos, a free audio book or any other offer materials that will have the effect of creating a closer and deeper relationship with your readers.

"Getting new customers and keeping them is the most critical aspect to developing a business with solid staying power"

As an example, one of our associates wrote in one of his books about an experience he had while shooting a video with his iPhone. He said that the result he was able to achieve was totally indistinguishable from a similar video shot with a $4,000 video camera. The point that he was trying to make was that his reader actually had a quality video production studio in their pocket! He concluded his message by telling his reader to text their email address to him to watch a side-by-side demo. As a result, he got their email address and phone number, which led to thousands of dollars in business.

It is important to note that the reason you need to have a "call-to-action" in your book is because the publisher of your book does not give you the contact information of your book buyer. As a result, you will need to incorporate strategies and tools that will drive your readers to you so that you can capture their contact information.

The "call-to-action" is the "how" and, the easiest and most efficient way to achieve this. Another of our associates also uses software that functions as a multiple "marketing machine" that literarily, by filling in the blanks and pressing a button, in 10 minutes can create a website, write copy, sells books, harvest leads, deliver content with email, mobile text and voice mail, and all done automatically.

Writing your book and promoting it properly is the foundation that will instantly create the kind of credibility that will help you sell your products and services easier and faster than any of your competitors. We have seen proof of this time and time over.

That's why as authors and business consultants ourselves, we always recommend to new clients or, to those existing business people who are trying to re-invent themselves, to write their story and make their passion come alive and let the world know who they are, and what you stand for.

Regardless of the content that is being written, the underlying objective is to create a trusting bond with the reader so that as an author and an authority in a specific field, whatever recommendations or products are being discussed in the book, they will be enthusiastically received and result in generating revenues. After all, would you rather do business with a "self-proclaimed expert" that hands you a business card or an author who is a published authority in their field and who hands you their book? Who do you think you will remember more?

Using Your Book for Publicity

Your book can also be used as the perfect way to get attention from the media, which would include radio shows, TV interviews and exposure to social media. Virtually every chapter in your book can supply information that can be used for a radio or TV interview or possibly for a speech or for a YouTube video.

It also might be perfect for content than can be used for a Podcast. Your book represents a marketing roadmap that will offer you a script and a formula for what to communicate to various audiences.

People who interview you will most likely pick the subjects they want to talk about from your book, which eliminates any doubt or confusion since you already are the expert on that subject.

If you own a local business your business is no longer confined to the local geography of where you live. It is amazing how many business owners do not see or realize the potential of globalizing or at least expanding beyond their local borders.

The Internet and mobile marketing, as discussed in earlier chapters, has changed the perception of how business is getting done these days. Unfortunately, because of the growing social media phenomenon, as well as the Internet and other digital outlets, competition has gotten tougher creating tremendous pressure on local merchants in their communities.

As a result, more and more business have begun to gravitate to the digital world in order to compete and survive. Yet, what angle or hook do they have that will distinguish themselves above their competition?

"Virtually every chapter in your book can supply information that can be used for a radio or TV interview or possibly for a speech or for a YouTube video"

Today consumers have many choices where they can purchase goods and services. Their purchasing habits are no longer confined to local geography. However, there is one common thread that all consumers share and that is the issue of "Trust". While trust is real, it is also a perception that is projected upon the public in the media. Businesses spend a fortune on generating the perception of trust in the marketplace.   When consumers feel the businesses and individuals they do business with are trustworthy, they buy and form a lasting relationship with them.

Understanding this fact so well is the reason why we recommend writing a book to all entrepreneurs who need or want more customers or clients.   We believe it is a unique and effective marketing angle.

Credibility and authority comes with being a published author and, with your book being properly promoted through the channels we have outlined here in our book, we are confident that "trust" will be your reward that will help toward monetizing your efforts. Your book will instantly help you to stand out in the crowd and have a distinct advantage over your competitors.

"There is one common thread that all consumers share and that is the issue of trust"

Knowing the typical questions that your prospects have consistently asked or have been concerned with in the past can be addressed and answered in your book. This will allow you to minimize or even eliminate in advance, any hesitation or resistance to product or service recommendations that you might be making in your book.

We thought we mention that some entrepreneurs who are engaged in the business of financial planning, investing, medical, healthcare, franchises, legal and multi-level marketing to name a few, have had serious concerns about writing and publishing books on their subjects because of the potential compliance or legal ramifications.

However, with a few exceptions, nobody or no business can prevent you from telling stories or writing about your personal life experiences or even giving advice. Writing a book is a marketing strategy that will work for you regardless of what business you are in.

Selecting the Content in Your Book

Let's face it; you can't fly an airplane unless you first learn how to fly. The same holds true that you can't publish, promote or profit from your book until you first figure out what you are going to write about, what your "hook" or angle is going to be, what the title and subtitle is going to be called or, what type of audience is going to be interested in your story?

Start by asking yourself the question " why do I do what I do" and how will it relate and attract new customers to my business? If you have trouble with this, don't worry. It may take a little time for you to figure it out but once it comes to you, the confidence that you will express to others will be authentic and trusting.

> *"First figure out what you are going to write about, what your "hook" or angle is going to be"*

Probably the biggest challenge that authors who are first starting out have is that they are not quite sure who their audience is, or might be. Of course, the answer will lie in correlating the content of your story to an audience that you know will appreciate the history and challenges that you were confronted with including your message on how you were able to deal with and finally resolve the controversial issues in your story. The "hook" or angle will be revealed in that message and will happily resonate with your target audience.

The secret of being a successful author is to have the ability to address your readers as if you were addressing each one individually; the sensation of having each reader feel like you are talking to them personally. Let your compassion be felt as you tell your story so that your readers empathize and are drawn to and act on your "call-to-actions" in your book.

You want the objective of your book to create a deep and trusting bond beyond what you have written so that they will be receptive to other of your product materials like videos, audio books, podcasts and consulting just to name a few.

Yet, as simple as this explanation is, there are thousands of struggling entrepreneurs out there that if asked who their perfect customer might be, usually the response is "everyone"! Of course that would be true if it were possible for those entrepreneurs to cite examples and show written letters of commendation from actual customers who have benefited from their products, services or advice.

However, if you were to examine those letters you would find a common thread between all those that did write in; having the same interests, and being members of the same audience with similar concerns and who had experienced a positive transformation by the content in the author's book.

It is clear that authors who write transformational stories that capture the heart of their readers or listeners, are the ones that that write the best books and have the most successful businesses.

The bottom line here is that your story has to be interesting to an audience that your experience has something in common with. Determine who best represents the reader or listener in the audience that you are writing to. Don't be general. Be specific.

If you are a musician writing a book or delivering a Podcast on the "10 easiest steps to learning chord progressions on a Piano", your target audience would not be readers or listeners who are interested in "Italian Recipes" or even musicians who play the saxophone, unless they play piano to.

The title and content of your book is directed to an audience that is most likely new to the piano seeking an easy way to learn chords. As you can see, by creating an "Avatar" or a hypothetical person who represents the target market you are going after, this will allow you to cut to the chase and design your marketing strategy around attracting readers and listeners from that audience.

Depending upon the category of the content in your book you might also want to include the age, gender, ethnicity and education of your Avatar. One way of creating your Avatar is to think about the best customer you have ever done business with. Who was he or she? What was their personality like? Were they inclined to give you referrals?

Were they repeat customers or were they ongoing clients in need of the various services that you offer? Once you have an overview of the characteristics that make up your Avatar, the next step is easy. As mentioned earlier, you can now begin to "Perform" your book by simply first writing out 10 or 15 questions that you think your Avatar might ask you about the subject matter in your book.

"One way of creating your Avatar is to think about the best customer you have ever done business with"

Once this preliminary preparation is completed, you now have a framework to start writing by elaborating on each answer to the questions that would be most likely asked. As mentioned earlier, according to best-selling author Mike Koenigs, who uses this method in preparing to write his books, it only takes about 2 ½ to 4 hours of recorded content to produce approximately, 120-140 pages of copy simply through a combination of questions and answers. That equates to about ½ day of providing stories related to the questions that were proposed.

The three big mistakes people make when they write books that are unsuccessful is that they think that their book has to contain a lot of facts, charts and be lengthy. This is not only boring but also a formula for disaster because in reality, most readers do not have the patience or time to read a lengthy tell-all book.

"Books that contain the most effective content tell stories of transformation"

When your book shares strong, personal emotional stories coming from a perspective that is unique, it will result in being better than any amount of facts and figures. What is interesting is that most people have enough material in them to write several books just with the information that they can derive simply by asking questions and getting answers from their friends, prospects, customers or their clients.

Whether you are, or are not a professional writer, is not relevant because the chances are that you are not. However, are you a storyteller? Once you have selected the audience that you are targeting you will want to resonate with your readers by getting their attention through telling the story of who you are and how you became interested in your occupation, hobby or avocation and what kind of obstacles or problems that you faced and what you did to overcome them and how it has changed your life and how your message and recommendations could help your readers in their journey.

Once your book is completed, combining a great title, subtitle and compelling cover is an easy formula designed to get attention, grab that target audience and sell your book.

Publishing Your Book

The partners that you will have in this journey like Amazon, Apple and Barnes and Noble to name a few, will give you a personal author website that gives you a high SEO ranking, sell your book and pay you 70% commission or more and give you the credibility and an equivalence of an Amazon and Apple endorsement.

They will also give you a place to post you're your social media link, including book signing and event schedules, a gallery for pictures and videos of you which can also include your books, your clients and television appearances.

It's all <u>free</u> and virtually social proof. We have found that the books that contain the most effective content tell stories of transformation. Readers find it interesting on why you do what you do and how you've used what you have learned and applied to help yourself. This kind of content connects with your reader, in a hope that it will relate to his or her own life experiences.

Even though the publishing industry as a whole is still a very big business, Amazon is quickly approaching 40% of all book sales worldwide as authors can now publish their books in days or weeks instead of years. In addition, authors can keep all the money rather than pay royalty fees to book agents. If an author knows how to properly promote their book and themselves through all the media outlets that have been described earlier in this book, they can make a great living by creating a "backend" revenue stream through selling their products and services.

When you finish and are ready to publish your book by uploading to Amazon as an example, you will start receiving royalty payments every 30 days after it begins selling. Amazon will put the money directly into your account. When you publish to other platforms like Bookbaby, Nook and Barnes and Noble to mention a few, you will start to earn even more.

While receiving royalties on your book is a potential income stream, do not lose sight of your overall objective, which is to really monetize the effort that can result from writing your book. In that regard, your "Call-to-Action" segments that appear at the end of each chapter will harvest your reader's emails and help sell various products that you offer directly or through your affiliate network.

You will also be able to invite your readers to tune into your podcasts for continuing information related to the content in your book. Some authors, who understand this objective, will initially price their book at the lowest possible rate while hoping for their book to generate the more lucrative results of generating leads and product or service sales. Over the long term, the value of the lead could be worth substantially more than the royalty. As an example, with an audience that is receptive to the content in your book and who responds to your "Call-to-Action" segment, each lead could be potentially worth $25-$100, more than the $0.35-$7.00 royalty.

Your Book as an Audio Version

Another way of making money with your book is to create an Audio version and sell it on iTunes or Audible.com or Amazon's audio store. Book listeners are usually different than book buyers. They like listening on their iPhones, tablets and computers or in their cars. With that in mind, there is a program on Amazon called Audio Creation Exchange (ACX), which can help sell the audio version of your book.   When someone downloads the audio version of your book they will pay you a commission of 40% to 50% or higher.   As a result of someone downloading your audio version and becoming an Audio book subscriber, ACX will pay you a bonus of $50.

It's amazing! ACX will give you <u>free</u> Audible Amazon and iTunes distribution instantly with tremendous visibility. While it's a way to reach more people in a very personal way, you always own and control the content and can take it down anytime you choose.

The great thing about creating an audio version of your book is that you do not need to come up with new content for your book. All you have to do is read and record the content and suddenly, you have a new product that can be sold online; a product like your e-book or paperback version that can also be a lead generator for you.

"Book listeners are usually different than book buyers, they like listening on their smartphones, tablets and computers or in their cars"

It is important to note that inside Amazon's ACX program, if you desire, there are many names of producers and audio voiceover talented people that can help to narrate your book for you. A very effective "Call-to-Action" give-a-way bonus is to offer your book readers a free audio copy of your book if they text their email address to you.

Making Money from Affiliate Marketing Sources

Although touched upon earlier, another great business category to generate ongoing revenues is through "Affiliate Marketing".

Companies who offer products and services will offer you a commission for linking your readers to their websites in order to buy their products and services that resulted from your recommendations that were made in the "Call-to-Action" sections of your book or in your videos or podcasts.

It is a "pay for performance" business model. As an example, once you have set up an Affiliate relationship with Amazon, they will pay you a commission if you send one of your readers to Amazon with a special link that they will provide to you. The good news is that there are lots of great companies with great products that you can establish an Affiliate relationship with. For any of the goods and services they offer that you recommend, those companies will be happy paying you a commission.

Let's face it; a book is often the ultimate credibility piece to a reader who is absorbed in what you have written. If you are making a recommendation of a product or service in your book, there is an excellent chance your reader will follow your recommendation and click on the Affiliate link that you have provided in that particular "Call-to-Action" segment.

"Another great business category to generate ongoing revenues is through Affiliate Marketing"

Obviously, you will want to first seek out companies with products and services that are relative to the content in your book in order to establish an Affiliate relationship in advance of publishing your book.

In order to generate traffic, leads and affiliate sales, one of our best selling authors from our community of book publishers creates chapters in his book about a specific strategy and tactic. He writes about the result and outcome that he knows his reader is going to be interested in.

At the end of each chapter he tells the reader that they can get a free copy of a video that demonstrates the step-by-step tactic being used in that strategy to achieve the results. Obviously, this can work for entrepreneurs in the financial industry, weight loss, nutrition, consulting or any other product or service industry.

This is a strategy that generates the kind of motivation that will create a reason that makes sense for the reader to give you their contact information in exchange for receiving the valuable instructional materials or videos that you are offering. In order to create a steady stream of income as a result of publishing your book, you only need one or two of the marketing ideas outlined here in these pages to be successful. Pick one or two of them and get started.

Summary of Key Benefits to the Book Publishing Strategy

• *Package your ideas, expertise, know-how, wisdom, into sharp looking little book.*

• *Amazon, Apple's iTunes and others will sell your book for free and pay you 70% commissions.*

• *The most popular social media networks will promote and market the content in your book for free and make you accessible to 73% of the world!*

• *Your book content can be turned into Audio books, podcasts, videos, articles, slides, pictures, and articles.*

• *Your book can lead to paid consulting assignments for you.*

• *Your book can give you access to the media, interviews and celebrity status with an opportunity for speaking engagements and media panel discussions.*

• *You can passionately brag, talk and extol the virtues about your products and services.*

• *Anyone who buys your book has proven to you that they are interested in your content and will be most likely to act on your "Call-to-Action" recommendations.*

• *You can offer incentives to your readers in order to receive their name, email address, phone-number and physical address so they will be receptive to buying your products and services.*

LEARN MORE ON HOW BOOK PUBLISHING GETS YOU MORE CUSTOMERS!

Register for the FREE book updates, training videos, livecasts, video gear guide and access to our Digital Marketing Mastery Training Portal.

Visit http://0s4.com/r/MRK3B4 or
(Http://www.riseabovethecloud.net) or
text **Bookbonus** to 58885 or
text your email address to 1-805-601-8001

STRATEGY 4: PODCASTING MARKETING

Overview

"17% of US adults listened to a podcast during the past month." -
Statista (2015). In 2014, there were 1 billion podcast subscriptions.

What exactly is podcasting? According to Paul Colligan, one of our Nation's top experts on the subject, he has broken down the definition and meaning as creating <u>audio</u> or <u>video</u> content that is made available online for easy, on-demand consumption as well as subscription- based delivery.

Podcasts can be accessed on any device such as an iPhone, Android, Computer, iPad or any other kind of tablet. Listeners or viewers can access your podcast on any device they own including their car radios.

As an Industry, "Podcasting" has been growing since 2006. Since then, and especially since the introduction of smartphones, more and more individuals are listening to podcasts than ever before as the trend continues to increase with the growing subscription rate of new smartphones and other mobile devices.

According to "Statista", the Statistic Portal, the information in their survey taken in 2015 showed the share of the US population that had listened to an audio podcast in the last month from 2008 to 2015 found that 17 percent of US adults had listened to a podcast during the month leading up to the survey. Now utilizing inexpensive and rapid Internet connectivity, mobile users, regardless of their devices, can listen to podcasting content of their choice, anytime, anywhere that they choose.

While people have the ability of viewing a variety of content on demand on YouTube or on the Web, they are not always in front of their computers. By comparison, most people today usually have access to their phones 24 hours a day, every day of the week, carrying them in their pockets or purses and then, upon getting into their cars, connecting their smartphones via their Bluetooth connection.

With the ability of having high speed connectivity, people can now access their favorite podcasts the moment they are interested in listening without having to log on to their computers and sync with their phones. This has all been made possible because of today's technology. Another factor, which is important is, people have been getting used to obtaining their content over the Internet through popular online service providers like YouTube, Netflix, Hulu, or Amazon's Kindle.

You, as a provider of content in a specific category, can be an expert in that field but the mainstream media is not likely to pick you up. Traditional media sources like television or radio are not likely to be an avenue to distribute your content. However, with today's technology and the availability of a free distribution channel like YouTube, you can create your own quality television show, at little cost, and be up and broadcasting within a day. Depending upon the quality and importance of your content and the size of the audience that you develop as a result, it is possible that the mainstream media could pick you up.

As the rise and popularity of on-demand programming continues, broadcast television is beginning to lose its hold. Netflix is surpassing the content generated by Broadcast and Direct TV as they are now logging more content views in special programs. It appears that the convenience factor is winning as technology is now on an even par making podcasting realistic as well as practical and reasonable.

While Podcasting has been around for a while, it is only now that the mainstream market of listeners are coming to it and finding it is easier to consume content than ever before. Acquiring content from the Internet is very exciting and useful because of how it is found and presented. Let's face it, now is the time to get involved if you want to be part of something that has a huge upside potential.

"With today's technology and the availability of a free distribution channel like YouTube, you can create your own quality television show, at little cost, and be up and broadcasting within a day"

Now that technology has met up with the convenience factor, technology is no longer a psychological barrier of getting content from the Internet. Smartphone access to the Internet is easy, fast and cheap. Service providers like Amazon, Netflix and Hulu are rapidly overtaking mainstream media and the publishing industry. What is so great about this is that you can be part of this trend. Podcasting can help you establish yourself as an expert in your field.

You can now take advantage of the fact that technologic and psychological barriers have and, are continuing to lift making podcasting viable and profitable. With Podcasting as a rapidly growing industry, now, is a good time to get started and become part of it.

Reasons for Podcasting

According to Podcasting Guru Paul Colligan, there are really only three reasons to Podcast. He calls them the three P's of Podcasting. Passion, Position and Profit!

If you want to present an idea or talk about a subject that you are passionate with, podcasting is an ideal platform to utilize. However, passion alone may not be enough. There must be passion with an end game leading to profit and generating that profit, can be achieved if you properly plan.

The second objective is to position yourself with the content that represents your category so that it will be appealing to the audience that you are targeting. With current technology, fortunately there is no longer a wait to publish your content any longer. If you have a great idea, or a subject you would like to talk about, you can do so and then simply click the publish button and within moments your expressed thoughts on the subject matter you just discussed will become available worldwide to stream and download to any mobile device, with no distribution challenges.

"Podcasting can help you establish yourself as an expert in your field"

The problem of marketing and distributing products is a challenge that every business, big or small, faces. However, podcasting does address both of these. It is a great way to engage and identify with your listeners. Again, as mentioned earlier, if the delivery of your content is properly planned, your listeners will buy your books or your audio programs or any other service you are offering.

With that in mind, creating a strategy that will allow you to generate a _profit_ from your podcasting is the third and most important objective, as it will ultimately lead to your financial success as a podcaster. As you begin, develop the kind of strategies that deal with all the elements of passion, position and profit. Determine what your passion is about and incorporate podcasting as your marketing vehicle to distribute your content to your audience. Position yourself to be the expert or go-to person within your field of expertise. Most of all develop an effective strategy and delivery to profit from your Podcasting effort.

Equipment Used by Podcasters

What kind of equipment will you need? The first item you will need is a microphone to broadcast or record your audio. Of course, the microphone in your smartphone may be good enough. However, there are many brands of USB microphones that are highly recommended that you can buy economically on Amazon.

While it does not have to be a fancy Mic, keep in mind, the better and clearer the quality of your sound is, the better your podcast information will be received. As marketing specialist Mike Koenig has said, _"you never have a second chance to make a first impression."_ In the final analysis, the quality and timeliness of your content will be more important than the quality of your podcast.

Should you decide to make video a part of your podcasting efforts, you will need a video camera. Fortunately, you have one on your smartphone, which can be used since the quality of the video camera and microphone on smart phones these days actually work very well. However, there are many affordable, high-definition video cameras available on Amazon should you want to step up and produce a higher quality of video.

However, keep in mind, audio podcasting reaches many more people than a video podcast because there are many more venues where the content of an audio podcast can reach and be heard. If you are planning to initially podcast text for an ebook or a PDF format, before you invest in a video camera, the only equipment you will need is your computer and whatever word processing software you are using.

The most popular format for text-based podcasting is PDF files since all of the Google formats can export them. As a result, many podcasters have switched to Google Docs / Google Drive because there is no cost to host online content or for any collaboration.

Producing Content

You are mistaken if you think producing perfect content the first time you try will come out as you hoped. You are going to need audio and/or video editing software. One of the more popular recommendations for editing audio recording software is Audacity because it will work on all operating systems, which include, MAC, PC or Linux.

The good news is Audacity is completely free! However, if you own a MAC, you can use "Garage Band" an excellent audio editing program that comes with the computer. While there is other audio editing programs out there covering a range of prices, you should go with what you may already be familiar with to create and manage your podcast.

Once again, if you own a MAC, for video editing you can use "iMovie", a free program that comes with the computer. If you own a PC, Sony Movie Studio will work great for editing video on your computer.

Once your podcast is created and saved, you will want to distribute it online in a downloadable format. In order to do that, you will need an online media host as well as an "RSS Feed" that will allow your podcast content information available to all providers like iTunes, Stitcher and others.

Fortunately, there are systems that can do everything for you. But remember, your media host and your RSS provider need to be podcast compliant. To avoid wasting time when selecting a service provider that you might have found on Google, be sure to ask the one you select if their hosting service supports and meets the compliance requirements for podcasting.

Creating a podcast takes three simple steps; a microphone if you are just going to record audio, a video camera if you are going to do video podcasting and word processing capabilities to manage your text. Basically, all three items can be found on your computer at no cost! However, as indicated earlier, you will need someone to create your RSS feed and a hosting service that supports podcasting. While not all services can do this, be sure to qualify whom you select to make sure they meet the requisite approval.

Here is the big question every podcaster would like to know; how do you make money as a podcaster? While passion, as discussed earlier, lasts only so long, you should be able to make money podcasting. Successful podcasters in the community say that there are three ways to make money as a podcaster:

- **Indirect Method**

This method occurs when you are able to leverage the content of your podcasts or a published book predicated on the same content. This method might result in an invitation to speak at a large function or even appear on "Talk Radio" or television. As a result, your audiences will be inclined to buy or subscribe to whatever you are offering including being hired as a consultant in your field. However, this is not necessarily a good, long- term plan because the strategy is unpredictable as compared to other marketing methods. A better approach and second way to monetize your podcasts would be:

- **Direct Method**

Your goal here is to make money directly from your podcasts. As an example, you can make money from Ads that you place in your podcasts. However, you would need a sizable audience to make any serious money. What has proven to be a better approach is incorporating commissionable Ads in your podcasts. With an interested audience that you created as a result of your content, you will find them to be receptive and willing to spend money on what you are sponsoring through your "Affiliate Marketing" ties because of the diversity of products that are relevant to the content in your podcasts. Utilizing Affiliate Ads to the right kind of audience will give you substantially higher commission returns than the average Podcast.

- **Sponsorship**

Unlike other options, for each Ad that is being viewed, you get paid. The difference is with a commission; you get paid when someone buys something from you as a result of having listened to your podcast. With "Sponsorship", a company will offer you an amount of money to be your "Lead Sponsor". Essentially, the company is buying visibility and access to your audience.

This type of relationship can be either big or small and works well when your audience is the same audience that is interested in the same product or products of your sponsor.

Of course the best approach is selling your own product or products. Once your audience has listened 10 or 15 of your episodes, with your ever-increasing credibility, they most likely are ready for whatever you have to offer.

Making Money with Your Podcast

You now have a wonderful opportunity to make money through an integrated strategy utilizing an email newsletter and webcasts to promote both physical and virtual products. You are now in a great position to grow and have a terrific presence as a podcaster. However, an integrated strategy is more than a podcast. You must make your content available in many ways like a live event or on a blog a newsletter or a YouTube video or any other outlet that there is an audience.

"A company will offer an amount of money to be your "Lead Sponsor". Essentially, the company is buying visibility and access to your audience"

One of the prime benefits of podcasting is that your audience can consume your content anywhere, any time, and anyhow they choose.

Some of the other venues mentioned earlier might even present an opportunity for new listeners who might have never heard you before and who will now become enlisted as new members of your growing audience.

Podcasting in itself is not an end-all. It is a multi-faceted platform that can instantly broadcast and distribute your content to any device, regardless of where it is in the world! It is an effective and important way to build a solid relationship with your target audience. Another advantage is that Google loves podcasts. According to some of the most successful podcasters they say, while video podcasting on Google takes a little more work than creating web pages, if you are providing consistent content, from a SEO standpoint, Google will notice this and a second listing inside Google might result.

Before you begin you will need to decide whether the approach you use will be direct, indirect or that you are going to utilize the integrated method for making money with your podcast. If you don't have a plan to use the direct method, make one in advance before you begin.

Should you decide on using the integrated method as described earlier, make sure all of your components for your podcast are in place as this method requires a variety of content. In addition, you will also want your podcast to take advantage of increasing your SEO capabilities.

Uploading and Publishing Your Podcast

There are basically two steps to creating and publishing your Podcast:

- The first is to create your media file, which can be an audio, video or text file.

- Your next step is to upload your media file to the Internet along with your RSS feed.

Creating your media file should be simple. Use a delivery platform that you are already familiar with. Remember, your content must be the center of what you focus on.

Audio files for Podcasting are created as .MP3 files. Videos are saved as .MP4. Text files are usually saved as .PDF files. While other file formats are available, there is no guarantee that all media players can support other file formats. Keep in mind you can always hire professional people who specialize in editing media files. There are many people who do this and you will find their services to be rather inexpensive.

As discussed earlier, after you create and upload your media you will need a hosting site that will allow you to post and stream your podcasts. It is important to note that whomever you select, make sure that you retain ownership of your content. You do not want the hosting company you select to own your content. Make sure retention of your content is understood up front or in any written documents that are required to be signed.

Many of our customers have asked which companies we might

recommend. In that regard, we are happy to provide the names of a few companies that we have found to be reliable in uploading media files and podcasts including the RSS feeds.

Based upon the podcasting system that you choose, the RSS feed is automatic and is the application that broadcasts to everyone that there is a new episode. That's all there is to it. You now have created and published your podcast!

The great thing about creating a podcast now is how inexpensive it is as compared to what it might have cost several years ago when you would have had to reserve time in a broadcasting studio, hire an audio engineer and pay everything by the hour.

Today, with current technology, creating podcast is as simple as recording yourself, and calling it in. It is like leaving a voice message. Just connect a microphone to your computer and record. Once you have your content you can edit out any unwanted verbal errors or noises. You can even add music. Once your podcast is recorded to your liking, you can save it as an .MP3 file.

Although there are several Apps for your smartphone that you can use for recording, as mentioned earlier, we recommend using the free, "Audacity" software to record your podcast directly to your computer. If you want the quality of your audio to be really good, use a good USB microphone with the Audacity software.

For real clarity, we suggest applying an audio filter also known as a compressor, which will result in making your podcast sound better. However, remember the content of your podcast will always be more important than the quality of how it was delivered.

Lastly, if you feel uncomfortable in setting up your podcast recording yourself, there are people you can hire that will come to your place of business and set up the recording for you.

Hosting Your Podcast

When it comes to hosting your podcast -- using Google, Bing, or whatever search engine you prefer will work. Be sure to check out the individual reviews of those companies you find and also keep in mind that many hosting companies with unlimited bandwidth do not extend this to podcasting. Be sure that the one you select does allow for podcasting and that you own your content.

Another factor to be sure of is, does the hosting company that you select have sufficient "Up Time" that allows for podcasting? The last thing you want to happen is having your podcast shut down in the middle of a broadcast, which would most likely create a negative experience with your audience. This is why we recommend caution when selecting a podcast host. Remember, a Web host and a Podcast host are not the same.

Traditional Web hosts with unlimited bandwidth do not have podcasting compatibility. Should your audio or video podcast really go viral, causing a spike in bandwidth costs, without a specific agreement allowing such an increase, they are most likely to shut you down resulting in losing your audience and the credibility that you worked so hard to achieve. As an example, this situation could occur if your podcast was seriously and heavily being downloaded as a result of being featured on iTunes or other popular media venues.

With respect to you uploading your podcast, the process is extremely easy. The podcasting systems on your MAC or PC will allow you to upload to a Website page form any desktop. While some might require an FTP program, the good news is that there are many FTP programs, readily available and most of them are at no charge.

There are some Apps that can automatically upload your podcast. One leading podcaster uses "Bossjock Studio" which allows you to record your podcast right on your iPhone or iPad and then instantly publish your content on the publishing media that you had selected. However, keep in mind, as easy as this process is, you can always hire someone who is familiar with this whole process.

If you would like a list of reliable hosting companies or other App companies. Just email your request to info@mobiledata360.com and we will email you back a recommended list that you can research and select from.

Where Will my Audience Come From?

One of the main questions always asked is "How does my audience get notified or updated when I create and publish my new podcast episode"? Of course, the misconception here is that you will have to notify a variety of distribution channels, every time you record a new episode.

The answer is simple, you don't! Once you have submitted your first podcast to the right directories, each time you update your RSS feed with a new podcast, on your behalf, the directories will automatically notify everyone. This is the beauty of podcasting.

However, this does not mean you don't have to make an effort to market your new podcast. You still have to market your content and get people to subscribe so that you continue to retain older subscribers while attracting new ones. Getting people to subscribe to your podcasts is solely your responsibility.

One of the most critical things about podcasting when you start is maintaining a regular and consistent relationship with your subscribers. Once your audience has identified themselves as listeners and followers of the content in your discussions, they are going to want continuity in the underlying theme of your podcasts.

In that regard, setting a regular time during the day or evening of the week for your podcasts allows your listeners to look forward to hearing your podcasts with regularity because of the predictability of the broadcast time they will have come to expect.

Developing this kind of audience intimacy should be the goal of every podcaster because it is the best and most efficient way that monetizing a podcast can be achieved. Because of the trust you will have earned, in the right context, you will be able to sell a variety of products and/ or services that you feel might be of interest to your subscribing audience. After all, we assume you want to make money with your podcasting efforts?

Who is your audience? Are they daily listeners? You could set aside one day to make a series of podcasts and distribute them throughout the week, one day at a time. Or, you could create a weekly or bi-weekly podcast.

Much will depend upon the nature of your content. However, whatever time frame you decide upon, be regular and consistent with your delivery so that it is predictable to your audience. Most importantly, if you are delivering new episodes every Thursday morning at 7:30AM, while your audience is driving to work, remember, not everyone has a program that will remind them or notify them of your new episode.

The best way to notify or alert your audience is through interacting with them through emails, text messages or phone calls, whose names and numbers you regularly harvest through your "Call-To-Action" bonus segments in your podcasts. This approach is personal, popular and powerful because of the directness affect that it has.

When it comes to the broadcast media like the radio and television industry, their listeners and viewers are conditioned to their shows being broadcast on specific days and at specific times.

This is why we feel for creating and retaining a long term audience and branding that is sustainable, if you schedule your podcasts at regularly scheduled times your audience will trust and respect you more because of the similar discipline you are incorporating in your broadcast scheduling.

How often you plan to release new episodes of your podcast will depend upon the preferences of your audience. Whatever time frame you decide upon, be sure to be consistent. Make sure you give your audience ample notification time before each episode. Think of producing your podcasts like it was one of your audience's favorite radio or television shows.

Although, for most people the term "Podcast" means free, there are certain podcasts providers that charge a fee. The problem here is that with so many podcasts being available for free, the majority of podcast listeners would find it difficult to pay for content that they are already receiving for free!

Yet, while we do not anticipate a rapid change in that direction, recently, there has been some movement toward paid content particularly in the financial services industry where special subscription membership is required as part of a larger and more comprehensive platform which may include investment advice and timely stock recommendations.

As discussed earlier, this type of podcast would fall under the "Integrated" model of podcast monetization. The important thing is to determine, through observing what other successful big name podcasters are doing is how to emulate them. Ultimately, your content and the audience market you create as a result, will determine which marketing method will provide the best financial results.

Most of the top rated podcasts on iTunes are radio shows, television shows and movies. This is because the podcasters of these shows have learned to keep their ratings high by continuing to request their viewers to subscribe to their podcasts at the conclusion of each of their shows.

- Several of the most successful podcasters have suggested that in order to get and maintain a high rating you have to obtain a lot of subscriptions in the shortest period of time. Although un-official, they have said that 80 percent of your score will be based upon how many subscribers you were able to get in the last twenty-four hours.

One way to accomplish getting to the top of the iTunes list is to contact your current list of subscribers and prospects and make it beneficial for them to subscribe to your podcast at a specific time. As an example, you could offer certain bonus material to the first 100 subscribers that sign in at that prescribed time.

The lesson here is to be sure that you never stop asking people to subscribe to your podcasts. In order to build a regular list of subscribers, it must be part of a continual educational process. Be sure that in every email or marketing collateral and social media that goes out to your customer or prospect list you include the statement "Please Subscribe to my Podcast" This action must be part of your ongoing marketing effort. You want your audience to know, like and trust you. Your regular podcast and the content that it contains will become the key link between you and your audience. It will build and enhance your credibility.

In order to become one of the 10 podcasts on iTunes it is estimated that you will need, on average, between 200-300 subscribers over a course of two to three hours. You will need to accomplish this through your ongoing marketing efforts in obtaining a reliable and continuous stream of subscribers.

This can be achieved by getting your audience involved with you; having them engaged by you asking questions and rendering advice or simply telling them what to do. While good reviews on iTunes are important, they may have no direct impact on your rating. However, your good iTune reviews will more than likely help to boost your subscriber list which ultimately is more important.

In any event, you will want your podcasts to stand out in comparison to your competitors. This of course will be dependent upon how well you market and promote your podcast. In that regard, your first consideration should be the album art that you plan to use.

Creating Your Podcast Avatar

We recommend that you create the image that you want to project even before you record the first episode of your podcasts. You will want to create or hire a graphic artist to produce a stunning and outstanding look to your podcast art as a compelling enticement for an audience to subscribe to your podcast.

Another standout feature will be the quality of your content and it's description and keywords that will assist in the search engines finding and ranking you. Use terms and keywords that your audience is likely to search for. If none of your keywords ever come up in iTunes during your audience's search they will not know that you even exist! That would be true of course anywhere else as well. In order for your audience to subscribe to your podcasts they must be able to find you.

As mentioned earlier, good reviews in iTunes are important in the development of a growing subscriber list. It only makes sense that when combining good iTunes reviews with outstanding graphic art and quality content that it will lead to a sure-fire way to standout among your competitors. They might even subscribe without having ever listened to your content as a result.

You will also want to document your reviews from listeners at the conclusion of one of your episodes by asking them, "If they enjoyed your show, to please go to iTunes and give you a good review". This is particularly effective if you have had an opportunity to actually speak to members of your audience.

You should also try and generate the same kind of support outside of iTunes like on Facebook, Twitter or other social media platforms. The fact is podcasts go extremely well with social media. iTunes, Facebook and Twitter are very well aligned together. Each time you do a podcast episode, be sure to immediately share it with all social media outlets.

As we have mentioned several times earlier in various context, your podcast descriptions must accurately represent the content that your audience is listening to. It also must be presented in a way that will enhance your traffic derived from Internet search engines.

Finally, an aggressive and effective marketing effort designed to gather both internal and external reviews, will help set you above all other podcast listings.

Getting listeners to your podcasts starts with your entry in the iTunes directory, which is a lot like the Google directory. When you log into the iTunes store, click on the "Podcasts" button located in the upper part of the navigation bar. When you are on the podcast page you will see the Podcast Quick Links section. Click the button that says "Submit Your Podcast" That's it! Simple enough?

With respect to your audience, keep in mind the average person does not go on iTunes to find podcasts on subjects that they are interested in. While the trend to listening to podcasts as a source of finding relative content is on the rise, it still takes a lot of "word of mouth" and other forms of social media to get the word out.

When it comes to your audience, the important distinction to remember is that your audience is not generally listening for a podcast that contains content that they may be interested in.

However, once they are aware that your podcasts contains content on subject matter that they are interested in, they most likely will be become interested in being subscribers to your podcasts.

Exposure to podcasts means connecting with your audience through every possible level of communication. Make it easy and simple for your audience to subscribe. Add "Subscribe to" buttons and links in your emails as well as each and every Web page on your Website.

We also advise visiting "StitcherRadio.com" to set up an account so that you can make your podcasts available on their platform. This will help you to continue to build an audience for the content in your podcasts.

With regard to building your audience, is the audience that you are trying to attract a good match for your podcasts? Is the audience that you are trying to attract the kind of people who would most likely want to buy your products or services? In that regard, we suggest logging on to iTunes and check with the various list of podcasts that might be presenting the same kind of content that you are or contemplating.

Of course the simplest way to find out is to ask your prospects if they would be receptive to listening to your podcasts. You do this by not asking them directly but through other forms of communication that solicits a response to an inquiry regarding if they would be interested in receiving free, timely content on their cell phone, tablet or computer.

Naturally, the subject matter would have to be conceived as very beneficial so preparing and presenting your inquiry, needs to be well put together and convincing. Once you understand what kind of benefits your audience is looking for, your podcasts should be designed around selling the "Sizzle" rather than the "Steak".

As an example: suppose your podcast contains content on the subject of business. If you asked people to subscribe to your podcasts because the subject is on business, they might find that subject too generic because there are many broadcast outlets that discuss business, most of which they don't have time to listen to.

However, if you were to appeal to the same group of prospects, requesting they subscribe to your business podcast because you will be discussing how to avoid the "7 biggest mistakes" that business people make when they are updating the design of their websites, that's a different story.

In this instance, you are offering a direct benefit for your audience to tune in to. By taking this approach you will have set yourself up for a series of 7 different Podcasts that include in-depth discussions on each of the mistakes concluding with a "Call-to-Action" to join as free subscribers to either your next live podcast or, to receive an audio copy or PDF file of subsequent podcasts on the same or similar subject.

Importance of Owning Your Own Content

Maintaining copyright ownership of your content is critical. While we are not rendering legal advice, what we do know, and you can verify this, the basic element of copyright law is that you own what you create and produce. That includes any content that you produce. However, some unscrupulous podcast hosts will try to assume ownership of your content by having you not knowingly sign it away at the time you enter an agreement for hosting your podcasts. Make sure you read the agreement before signing anything. Under no circumstances should you give up the rights to your podcast content.

At the same time, it is a very bad idea to use someone else's copyrighted material in your podcasts. This is your chance to stand out "above the cloud" by expressing your views and ideas and using original materials to support them. If you plan on adding music to your podcast, there are sites that offer Royalty Free music that can be used in podcasts. Make sure you have the right to use whatever you select in your podcast.

One thing you will be curious about is how well your audio broadcast will sound to the audience you have worked so hard to attain? Assuming they have just downloaded your episode and have plugged in their ear buds or turned on their car radio and tuned into your podcast, what will the sound quality of your podcast be like? Naturally, you will want to make sure that the sound quality of your podcasts is the best that it can be. You will want to eliminate as much background noise as possible.

While you can spend a lot of money on an expensive microphone, it is not necessary in order to create quality audio. There are many good inexpensive microphones at $100 and under that you can choose from.

Creating your Podcast

Once you have selected the microphone you want to use, before speaking into it, you will want to be as close to your microphone as possible. The reason for this is to eliminate any other background noises beyond the sound of your voice. Because you are so close to your microphone, you may experience hearing a "spitting" or "popping" sound.

To avoid this, you will want to use a special filter that will block out those irritating sounds. While they cost around $20 to $30 dollars, you can try and actually make your own. There are instructional videos on "Hand Made Pop Filters" on YouTube.

It is important to note that if you are working at home and you have children or pets, be sure there is no disturbance coming from them while you are recording your Podcast.

Also, depending upon the room you are recording in, be sure to avoid any echoing effect which can be caused be your sound reverberating or bouncing off the walls.

Usually, being close to your microphone and using some sort of popping filter will do the job nicely. However, you could look into using soft pillows or other type of material that could be used as baffling in the event you still are getting some sort of residual noise background.

You will also find that some of the recording programs that you will use like Audacity, which is one of the programs that we recommend, have the ability of removing residual noises. Check your recording when you are finished to see how much if any, residual noise needs to be removed. The chances are that following our advice as to the location of the microphone in close proximity to your voice and utilizing a popping filter, as mentioned earlier, will produce a clear sounding quality recording of your content.

When you are inviting a guest to interview, make sure they know the name of your show, the website address of your show and most importantly, what your show is about. It is important that you explain why you would like them as a guest on your show and approximately how long the interview will take place.

Because of scheduling conflicts, it is a good idea to offer at least several time slots for your guest to choose from. Once you have confirmed the date and time with your guest be sure to explain how the interview will be conducted. If you will be utilizing "Skype", make sure you provide applicable contact ID or phone numbers and be sure they know who will be initiating the call. Make sure you send out a follow-up reminder at least one week in advance if your interview is scheduled for more than a week or so in into the future. However, regardless of when it is scheduled, send out a final reminder the day before. When sending out reminders, be sure to include "Time Zone" information in all your confirmation correspondence.

To insure that things go smoothly, it is recommended that you send your guest a list of questions that you will be covering in advance of the interview. If there are any last minute changes in your time schedule or an unforeseen conflict, be sure to communicate with your guest right away and make sure that they confirm your message. It is important that you contact your guest on time. Make sure your interview does not exceed the time that has been allotted.

Assuming you will have previously conducted some preliminary background check on your guest, be prepared to introduce your guest to your listeners rather than having your guest introduce themselves, make sure you pronounce their name correctly. When asking questions, allow your guest ample time to respond without speaking over them or even answering the question for them. Avoid questions that simply allow for one-word answers. When products or services are mentioned during the interview, be sure to include a "call-to-action" opportunity for the listener to email and obtain more information on the product or service that is being discussed. This is important in order for you to gain access to the listener's contact information.

Recording a Podcast interview when the participants reside in two different locations may seem a little complicated but it is simpler than what you would expect. Basically, there are three current options to choose from. One of Skype's best features is their easy and free video calling. However, if you need to record a video interview, or would like to keep some personal conversations private, it's easier to record a Skype video than you might think.

Since Skype doesn't currently include support for recording video calls, there are presently plenty of plugins that you can use that will do the job. Just for your information if you did not know, a plugin is a piece of software that brings additional functionality to a particular application like in this case, recording Skype video calls.

However, there are two things to keep in mind when you record a call with Skype. Unlike Skype's video feature, which is free, you will find most video recorder plugins are not. Also, before doing any sort of call recording, you should notify the other people who are on the call that you are recording it. The laws vary by state and country so be on the safe side and ask for permission first before you record a call with Skype.

Most of the available video recording plugins offer a free trial period, after which you have to pay to continue using the program. The programs that come in a free version are typically limited, recording only up to five minutes of video. Here are some plugin options for Windows users. However, if you're using Windows 8 you should double check that these plugins will work with new OS.

Podcast Recording Equipment

The one full-featured, completely free option we found is called, "Free Video Call Recorder for Skype" from DVDVideoSoft. This program features three settings: record all sides (picture-in-picture), record other side only, and record audio only. Skype will automatically launch as soon as you start the recorder, and after choosing your setting, you can start your conversation and hit the record button. The program creates MP4 files from your video calls and automatically saves it in the directory you choose. A great hang-up feature automatically stops recording when the conversation ends. (Windows only)

"Pamela for Skype" comes in four versions: a free Basic version that gives you five minutes of video recording. The next three tiers all give you unlimited video recording for a price: Call Recorder ($20), Professional ($33), and Business ($53). Along with unlimited video recording, the pay versions provide extras such as conference call scheduling, voicemail management, and a podcasting feature that posts recordings directly to the Web. Pamela records Skype video calls in "WMV".

If you'd like to share the video recording widely, use RealPlayer's free video recorder to save it as a MP4 file. (Windows only)

The $30 "SuperTintin" plugin lets you record Skype video in four modes: picture-in-picture, side by side (each side occupies half the screen), remote only (only the other participant is recorded), and local only (only your side of the video is recorded). SuperTintin saves video calls as MP4 files. (Windows only)

The first few options are for Windows users only. What about MAC users? Here are a couple of options that you can use to record Skype video calls on a MAC:

"VodBurner" lets your record and edit your Skype video calls for creating and distributing video podcasts. The program saves videos as MP4 or WMV files suitable for sharing with others. After recording a Skype call, you can use VodBurner editing tools to trim the video, as well as add text captions, pictures, background music, and external video. You can upload your recorded video call to YouTube directly from the application. After a 14-day free trial, VodBurner costs $100. (Windows and MAC)

Another program for MAC users is, "Ecamm Call Recorder for Skype" This program lets you record in picture-in-picture or split-screen modes. The program saves recorded video files as QuickTime movies, which you can also convert to MP3 audio files in the application. Ecamm Call Recorder costs $20 after a seven-day free trial period.

The second option is a "Digital Hybrid" this is used to do audio recording over the phone. The way it works is that it takes a phone line and it processes and mixes the audio so that it results in generating the best recording sound. You can then talk into a quality microphone while you are talking to someone who is the phone. Basically, it is what the radio stations use in shows where listeners call in.
The third option is a lot more technical. It's called the "Mix-minus".

The way this program works is a certain person records on a quality microphone at their location. At the same time, from a different location, a different person records on their microphone.

Later, during post-production, the two audio recordings are edited in the studio. The way the mix is accomplished is, by taking a third recording of just the phone and then lining everything up based on what you see on the phone. The final step is to take out the phone piece, which will allow you to end up with a great recording.

This technique, while somewhat complicated at first, produces a great quality recording. Of course, remember, it is producing your content that is most important so if this last option seems all to complicated, there are cheap audio editors out there that you can hire at a reasonable price to do it for you.

Summary of Key Points to the Podcasting Strategy

- *Incorporate podcasting as part of your marketing strategy.*
- *How to determine and establish your audience.*
- *Create your avatar.*
- *Know the necessary equipment to create a podcast.*
- *Create the appropriate content for your audience.*
- *Determine the delivery platform of your podcast.*
- *How to publish your podcast.*
- *How to monetize your podcast*

FIND OUT MORE ABOUT HOW PODCASTING CAN MAKE YOU MONEY?

Register for the free book updates, training videos, livecasts, video gear guide and access to our Digital Marketing Mastery Training Portal.

Visit http://0s4.com/r/MRK3B4 or
(Http://www.riseabovethecloud.net) or
text Bookbonus to 58885 or
text your email address to 1-805-601-8001

STRATEGY 5: SOCIAL MEDIA MARKETING

An effective social media plan is vitally important if you are to successfully market your product or service to your customers. In today's marketing strategy, it is all about "engagement" with your customers.

Mike Paule can recall his first entrée into the world of social media when he first signed up for Facebook back in 2007/2008. His oldest daughter had moved on from MySpace and created a Facebook profile. Wanting to keep tabs on his teenage daughter and at the same time fascinated by this new technology he set up his own profile and was off and running (initially to his daughter's chagrin more than likely).

What started initially as a way for Gen-X and Millennials to communicate with one another (boosted in large part by the phenomenon of instant messaging with AOL), the social media phenomenon has spread rapidly to include many different platforms and expanded across age groups from young to old.

While initially a tool for people to communicate with each other and to form social circles, it has rapidly evolved into an important tool for business to connect with its customers. Historically, online marketing was fairly one-sided. Businesses pushed ideas out and consumers passively received them, but that has changed with the popularity and use of social media channels.

The largest player in this space is of course Facebook, which went from obscurity (Less than 100 million users worldwide in 2008) to

1.35 Billion users worldwide as of the 3rd quarter, 2014. Meanwhile, Twitter which few knew anything about 6 years ago has grown from less than 10 million active users monthly in 2010 to 63 million active users as of the 3rd quarter, 2014.

Within the business community, Linkedin has become popular, although still is mostly used as a networking tool. Other social media platforms that have risen in importance the past few years include Instagram and Pinterest.

A September 2014 survey of U.S. Internet users who use selected social networks reveals that Facebook is used by 71% of Internet users, followed by Linkedin and Pinterest at 28% each, Instagram at 26% and Twitter at 23%. (Source: Statista).

An effective social media plan is vitally important if you are to successfully market your product or service to your customers. In today's marketing strategy, it is all about "engagement" with your customers. You want your customers talking about your company and your products or services. It is through these conversations that you will drive brand awareness.

To leverage social media, you will want to:
- Build Relationships
- Listen to your market
- Promote your content
- Influence your buyers

Using Facebook in Your Marketing

We mentioned that Facebook is the most widely used social media platform so naturally it would be good to start there. Facebook remains popular but has become more of a pay to play model in recent months.

On Facebook, the objective is to acquire fans for your business page where you can post status updates, videos and photos to your timeline. Recent changes in Facebook make it more difficult for fans to see your content without utilizing the Facebook promotion opportunities through their paid advertising. On your business page, you have the opportunity to promote your page or individual posts through some very easy to use tools that Facebook provides.

For example, when we launched our new business website for MobileData360 at the end of 2014, we used the Facebook page promotion technology to obtain over 400 likes within a one week period at a very modest cost of less than $100.

Through some great targeting tools that Facebook provides, you can get quite specific in your target marketing by identifying your specific audience profile such as age, gender, location, interests etc.

You can utilize the Facebook promote system to make sure your target audience has the opportunity to view your posts. When promoting individual posts, the objective is to create user engagement by driving them to your Facebook business page and your website.

Creating Ads in Facebook is pretty simple and you can setup your campaigns in a matter of minutes.

Here are some tips you should keep in mind when setting up your Facebook business page:

- Create a compelling cover photo that showcases your business and what you offer. Make sure you use a relevant profile photo.

- Make sure you have a good description of your business in the about section and be sure to include a URL to your company website.

- Make sure you obtain the custom URL link that Facebook provides which you can cut and paste to your website or use in your emails, business cards and other communication. (E.g. http://www.facebook.com/mobiledata360)

- Pick the right category for your business page.

For maximum effectiveness of your Facebook marketing efforts, it is important to keep the content relevant and engaging, and to post on a regular basis. Be sure to use photos and videos whenever possible to increase user engagement. For example, you could use a link in a post to take someone to an opt-in page where you can provide additional free content in exchange for them providing their email address, or phone number.

"With the growing reliance on social media, we no longer search for news, or the products and services we wish to buy. Instead they are being pushed to us by friends, acquaintances and business colleagues" -Erik Qualman – Best-selling author of Socialnomics.

Using Twitter in your Marketing

Over 63 million people turn to twitter each day to talk about things that interest them. They may be interested in a trending topic, or to learn about the latest news, talking about day-to-day life, or interested in products or services such as what you offer.

Twitter is a unique form of social media in that messages are limited to 140 characters. Your tweets are your message and often include links to outside sites, articles or other content such as videos. Through the use of hash tags as a mechanism to index the content, you can quickly find information on any given subject by searching these keyword tags.

In Twitter, people will decide to follow you which means that 100% of your tweets will appear in their twitter news feed. Whether they read or not is a different challenge. Also, the life of a specific tweet is pretty short as new tweets come in to the followers' twitter feed the old tweets get pushed down in the list.

Twitter is a good tool to convey short messages to your audience and encourage engagement through links to other sites, such as your website, opt-in pages, sales pages, or other content that you provide.

As is the case for Facebook, you should provide a nice banner for use on your twitter page, and include a URL to your business website.

For maximum effectiveness, it is important to create tweets on a regular basis and in fact, it is not uncommon to create multiple tweets per day to stay relevant in your follower's twitter feeds. Unlike Facebook, it is common for business tweets to be repeated during the course of the day to make sure your followers see them.

Using Linkedin in your Marketing

Another social media outlet that is popular among business professionals is Linkedin. As previously mentioned, Linkedin is especially relevant for those that are in the business community and tends to favor business to business marketing more than business to consumer. Linkedin is also quite popular for those looking for career changes.

In Linkedin you create a profile and provide regular updates that are broadcast to your connections. You invite others to make a connection with you on Linkedin and once that connection is accepted, you now have access to their full profile and also the ability to see all of the connections of the others who comprise your network.

In addition, people create groups and pages on various topics, which you can subscribe to and then all the members of these groups can post and respond to posts within these groups.

Linkedin does support paid advertising and if you are particularly interested in marketing to specific business categories or segments, it can be a nice way to reach your audience.

What we have observed as long time Linkedin members is that often we get connection requests from people who are intending to solicit us for their various products and services.

Using Pinterest in your Marketing

One of the most visual platforms in social media is Pinterest. This platform has been gaining popular in recent years and tends to have a majority of users who are female.

When you sign up for Pinterest you will select all the areas you are interested in and once you select these, you will be able to follow posts in these categories. The one thing you will notice is how visual the interface is and as you drill down through the categories you will see the various pins related to specific keywords.

Pinterest users post visual items as pins (or a collection of pins known as boards). Effective use of this social media platform requires a little more creativity. Its use as an effective business-marketing tool is still somewhat subjective and it does require more effort to create visually engaging. However, if your business offerings cater to the creative minds, it can be an interesting portal to reach specific types of consumers.

Key to Effective Social Marketing

The important key to effective social marketing is to know your audience and find consistent ways to engage them on a regular basis.

One question that we get asked often is how do you create your content to use on the various social sites? One of our top suggestions is to repurpose content that you may have already created in Blog posts, whitepapers, slide decks, videos, checklists and podcasts.

By cutting up that content into small chunks you can create easily shareable content that will help keep your audience engaged.

The Content Marketing Institute recommends how often each type of content should be shared on your social channels:

Content that:

- Entertains – Post monthly
- Inspire – Bi-weekly
- Starts a conversation – Weekly
- Teaches how to do something – Twice weekly
- Provide Relevant Information – Three times weekly

It is important to give people a reason to share your content. Peer-to-peer sharing is the most powerful way to build your brand visibility since people will believe their network of peers versus a company's brand driven campaign.

A Nielsen Survey showed that only 33% of buyers believe what a brand has to say about itself. In contrast, the same study showed that 92% believe what their peers have to say about a brand.

You need to give people a reason to share your content. The top 5 motivators that make people share (According to Marketo) are:

1. Reputation
2. Access to something exclusive
3. Co-creation
4. Competition and winning
5. Altruism

The other important point is that you want to make sure you prompt people to share your message at the right time. Best practice is to include social sharing links before or after a piece of content. One strategy is to utilize a popup box that asks them to share as they are reading a blog for example. This technique can also be used after someone downloads a content piece.

A comprehensive social media strategy is important if you are to build your brand and engage your audience. It may take a little time to build your following but the benefits of a sustained social media presence will pay dividends to your business many times over.

Summary of Key Points to your Social Media Strategy

- *Establish which social media platforms are best to promote your brand.*
- *Understand the differences between the top social media platforms, such as Facebook, Twitter, Linkedin, Pinterest.*
- *What is the key to effective messaging using social media.*

FIND OUT MORE ABOUT EFFECTIVE SOCIAL MEDIA MARKETING?

Register for the free book updates, training videos, livecasts, video gear guide and access to our Digital Marketing Mastery Training Portal.

Visit http://0s4.com/r/MRK3B4 or
(Http://www.riseabovethecloud.net) or
text **Bookbonus** to 58885 or
text your email address to 1-805-601-8001

MARKETING AUTOMATION TOOLS

"Good marketing makes the company look smart. Great marketing makes the customer feel smart." – Joe Chernov

Thus far in this book, we have written about some of the top strategies that successful entrepreneurs are using to build more leads, engage their audience, and ultimately gain more customers.

We have discussed the importance of creating compelling video content to connect with your prospects and customers. We have shown how mobile marketing is used to reach your audience in a way that they consume content – namely on their smartphones and tablets. We have emphasized how the proper use of social media can engage a community in a manner that builds the reputation of your brand and encourages them not only to buy from you, but also to recommend to their own network of friends, family and associates that they should check out your products or services.

However, you may be asking yourself: These all sound like good strategies, but aren't they time consuming to carry through in the way that will maximize my success?

The answer is "it could be" if not for the advancement in marketing automation tools and techniques.

Let's look an example of a typical day in a social media manager for (Marketo), one of the organizations that provide marketing automation for larger B2B companies.

Typical Day for a social media manager

Posts

Twitter
- 1 post per hour from
- 4 influencer re-tweets

Facebook
- 3-5 posts per day

Google+
3-5 posts per day

Linkedin
2 posts per day

Pinterest
- 4-5 pins per week

Monitor
- Check Twitter, Facebook, and G+ for mentions or anything that needs a response

- Respond to comments, customer issues, questions etc.

- Monitor throughout the day

Promote and engage
- Think of creative ways to promote content, events, and engage fans using pictures, infographics, stats, memes, questions

- Track success of promotions using Marketo Marketing Software Influencer outreach

- Read influencer posts on Twitter and other blog feeds and comment

Blog
- Create blog posts

- HTML edit blog posts so they are formatted and ready to be published

Now, granted this is for a larger organization, but it is a full time job just to keep up with all the activity that needs to be done daily.

For most small business entrepreneurs, there isn't the time, or typically the resources to keep up with the demands of creating and distributing content and monitoring all the social media channels. This is where marketing automation comes to the rescue.

Before we get into more detail on marketing automation, let's define what Marketing Automation actually is?

Marketing automation is a category of software that enables users to streamline and automate the typical marketing tasks and workflows so companies can improve their operational efficiency and grow revenue faster.

The technology behind marketing automation is used not only by larger enterprises but has found its way into the small and mid-sized (SMBs) business market.

In fact, SMBs make up the largest growing segment in the marketing automation technology space (Source: Marketo).

Marketing automation platforms typically feature:

- Email Marketing
- Landing Pages
- Campaign Management
- Content Management
- Lead Generation
- Social Marketing
- CRM Integration
- Marketing Analytics

What marketing automation is NOT is a fancy name for email marketing, or a way to send spam. It is also not a way to deliver value without effort. A good marketing automation strategy integrates the right people, content, data and timing to support your sales efforts.

Marketing automation is actually not even a new concept. According to Google, the term was first used in 1980, gained traction in the late 1990s, peaking around 2004. Declined in usage for a few years until 2007 when it began its steady rise again. Today it's near its 2004 peak.

What has changed over the years is the advent of online tools that have made it much easier to implement and track the results of marketing campaigns using automation.

Many are familiar with some of the automation tools built in email marketing platforms such as Constant Contact, AWeber, MailChimp and others. These tools let you create and schedule email campaigns and allow your prospects and customers to automatically opt-in and out of specific campaigns.

However, effective marketing automation is much more than email. An explanation of how marketing automation works can be illustrated by discussing some of the tools we work with on a daily basis. The Pulse Network provides a set of cloud-based tools called Traffic Geyser Fusion. Using these tools, users setup a full marketing campaign to capture leads, communicate with their prospect using auto responder technology, deliver free or purchased content directly to the user, schedule and deliver social media posts on a predetermined basis, upload videos to various video sharing sites, measure campaign metrics and provide timely feedback on the marketing campaign's effectiveness.

Since a small businessperson needs to effectively manage their time and resources, the use of such technology is invaluable if you want to deliver the results that you seek from your marketing efforts.

Let us outline in a practical way how a marketing campaign can be setup to utilize these automation tools:

Let's say for example, that you are giving a presentation to a large group of people utilizing the classic method of PowerPoint slides. Inevitably while you give your presentation, people will be furiously taking notes and someone will ask (or certainly be thinking), wouldn't it be great if we could get a copy of these slides. This probably sounds familiar to you.

What you may have often seen, is a speaker say something to the effect "if you want a copy of my slides, please give me your business card after the presentation and I will get it out to you." The reality is that most people will not make the effort to walk up and hand the presenter their card so the response rate is fairly low with this approach.

A much better solution might go something like this:

Part way through the presentation, the speaker would say *"I see many of you taking notes and since I want you to be able to concentrate on what I am saying, rather than racing to scribble down a bunch of notes, so I am happy to provide a copy of my presentation to you, as well as some additional material to help you understand the (fill-in the topic here).*

I know that many of you have your mobile phone with you so please pull out your phone and text (example: strategy to 55885 (short code example). You will receive an automatic confirmation with a direct link to download the slides, and also some bonus material such as (provide your audience with a description)." Your bonus material might include an audio file of your presentation, a white paper, and access to videos on the subject etc.

Done correctly, the participation of the audience could be 60-80%.

Once that individual's email address or mobile number is in the marketing database, you will be able to provide additional messages in a pre-determined manner. Perhaps, you develop an automated campaign that once someone opts in to your list, they might receive a series of emails, or text messages over a period of time (perhaps days) which help develop them as a qualified lead for your products or service. This type of marketing can be quite effective.

According to research done at MIT, the difference between following up to a customer hand-raise in 30 minutes versus 5 minutes means the difference between a 100 exchange in the contact rate and a 21 exchange in the likelihood of actually qualifying that lead.

Another use of marketing automation is delivering your video or other content to video sharing sites automatically, instead of taking the time to upload it one at a time to each site. Using these tools, you could for example, schedule your video to be uploaded to YouTube, Vimeo and Facebook at a predetermined time. You would enter the information into the software once and it would automatically post your videos to all the sites – saving you valuable time and effort.

Where marketing automation technology is really helpful is in social marketing campaigns. You could use the tools to setup a connection to all the social media platforms you utilize (such as Facebook, Twitter, Linkedin, Google+, Pinterest etc.). Then you could write your post and add any additional files or links that you want to include. You would setup the schedule and frequency of when these posts should be made and the software will do the rest.

Imagine prescheduling all of your posts for the week and being able to take a mini vacation without worrying about having to login in to each social media platform and prepare your posts one by one.

With the use of marketing automation technology, you will be able to engage your audience, communicate with them as often as you like and monitor the results through advanced analytics.

We provided one example of how this technology is used, but it can also be used to capture interest on a subject by directing people to a landing page, where you can provide a short video and opt-in form for viewers to access additional content. Once the opt-in form is completed, you would use the email auto responders in the technology to immediately reply back to that viewer and provide the requested contact.

Marketing automation solutions are particularly useful for mobile marketing, since users have immediate access to reply to your offer by texting or emailing their name to you to receive the promised content. You will find this is one of the best strategies you can employ to maximize your marketing efforts.

The adoption of marketing automation tools in your business will save you time and money and allow you to measure and optimize your marketing investments. All of this leads to faster revenue growth and greater profits.

If you are interested in learning more about this subject, we encourage you to visit us at **(http://mobilevideo360.com/videos)** where you will find a short video, which illustrates how this technology works to build your customer base.

DISCOVER HOW MARKETING AUTOMATION TOOLS SUPERCHARGE YOUR CAMPAIGNS!

Register for the FREE book updates, training videos, livecasts, video gear guide and access to our Digital Marketing Mastery Training Portal.

Visit http://0s4.com/r/MRK3B4 or
(Http://www.riseabovethecloud.net) or
text **Bookbonus** to 58885 or
text your email address to 1-805-601-8001

PUTTING IT ALL TOGETHER AND WHAT'S NEXT

I think we can agree that the marketing landscape has certainly changed dramatically over the past several years. The traditional method of marketing products and services has been transformed as consumers reach for their mobile devices in ever increasing numbers - literally hundreds of times a day to communicate and consume content with those in which they choose to engage.

As an entrepreneur or business professional, it is vitally important that you adapt to these changing conditions if you want to succeed with growing your business, adding new customers and even keeping the customers you already have.

In this book, we presented the key marketing strategies that have shown to be highly successful in creating results for businesses both large and small. We have discussed how the use of online video has proven to be a key customer engagement strategy and why short, targeted videos consistently provide great results.

We presented the latest in mobile marketing strategies, including a discussion of the importance of using various call-to-actions in your marketing campaigns, the use of SMS text messaging and fully-responsive mobile websites. Also, we provided details on how creating and utilizing a mobile app is important as a customer engagement tool and what a mobile app can do for your business success.

Establishing credibility is a key success factor, and one of the best ways to accomplish that is to publish a book which positions yourself as an expert in your field. It is easier and cheaper than ever to produce and publish a book and often this can be done in 90 days or less.

As a published author, you will find many opportunities to connect with your target audience, which will separate yourself from your competition. Imagine how your prospects and customers will view you if you are a "best selling" author on your subject. They will perceive you as the expert.

By producing content for your book or videos, much of this can be repurposed and turned into audio podcasts to further engage your audience. The podcasting market is growing steadily and it is easy and inexpensive to create your own podcasting channel and content, which is another way to reach your customers.

Many of the strategies that we have covered include the use of social media channels to help convey your message to your community of supporters. Social media is an important part of today's marketing mix and by creating the right kind of content, and staying consistent in your delivery of this content, you will be able to build your audience and subsequently increase your customers and sales.

As a small business owner, or marketing professional, you have a lot to do on a daily basis and therefore maximizing your efficiency in all of your marketing efforts is so important. Through marketing automation software tools, you are able to deliver consistent and timely content to the various video and social media channels -- helping deliver the results that you seek.

One of the objectives of this book was to provide you with a good overview of the tools and strategies that many are using to great success. However, it is not necessary to do everything at once, and you will want to target your efforts on those items that you feel most comfortable starting first and where you can expect to get the best results in the shortest amount of time.

Here is a list of the recommended strategies (in order) that you might consider as you move forward with implementation:

1. Create a Facebook, Twitter and Linkedin page for your business
2. Create a YouTube and/or Vimeo channel to post your videos
3. Create professional looking banners for these pages by using inexpensive outsourced resources such as www.fiverr.com.
4. Make sure you have an up-to-date website that is optimized for the mobile user.
5. Create and incorporate short, targeted videos into your website, email campaigns and social media posts.
6. Utilize call-to-actions for all of your marketing channels that include free content to your target audience in exchange for them opting in to your community.
7. Consider creating and self-publishing a book to establish yourself as the credible, go-to person in your market niche.
8. Create audio content to be delivered as podcast episodes, to be promoted on your social media channels and to your customers.
9. Create consistent and relevant social media posts, which provide real value to your prospects and customers, and ask them to share that content with others.
10. Automate your campaigns with marketing automation tools so that your content can be delivered efficiently, consistently and economically.

The key to any successful marketing program is that you have to actually **implement** your campaign. You might have the best strategy in the world for your marketing campaign but if you don't follow through with implementation, you won't see the results that you seek.

We have provided solid, proven strategies that will bring results, but it is important to take the time to learn how these strategies best apply to your business situation. Through education and follow-through you will achieve the success that you seek and be on your way to growing your customer base and increasing your profits.

It is time for our shameless plug. The authors of this book (Michael Paule and Shelly Dubow) provide training and consulting (online and in-person) to people who want to learn how to take the strategies presented in this book and turn them into more business and profits for you.

Throughout this book, we have provided links to additional bonus content where we provide a deeper dive into the subjects covered. One of these bonuses is a free 30-day trial membership to our Digital Marketing Mastery training portal where we will be offering weekly live training which will be recorded and available to you on-demand to watch at your convenience. Access this bonus content at http://0s4.com/r/MRK3B4.

We encourage you to take the time and learn how to effectively incorporate this knowledge to begin your own implementation plan. In the next section, we provide links to various resources that will help you get started.

RESOURCES/BONUSES

This book is intended to be interactive and provide you with the opportunity to learn more about the subjects presented.

We will be posting regular book updates and also providing bonus content to help you in your marketing efforts. We encourage you to take advantage of this FREE content by registering at http://0s4.com/r/MRK3B4

For convenience, we have provided multiple ways for you to join our community and take the first steps to better marketing results, more business and higher profits.

Multiple ways to register for your FREE Bonus Content

* Scan this QR Code to Register for the FREE Book Bonuses
* Or Visit http://0s4.com/r/MRK3B4
* Or Text **Bookbonus** to 58885
* Or Text your name & email address to 1 (805) 601-8001

Connect with us on Social Media

Facebook- http://www.facebook.com/mobiledata360
Twitter - http://www.twitter.com/mikep29
YouTube – http://www.youtube.com/user/mobilevideo360
Linkedin – https://www.linkedin.com/in/mpaule29

Visit our Website at http://www.mobiledata360.com

Made in the USA
San Bernardino, CA
22 April 2015